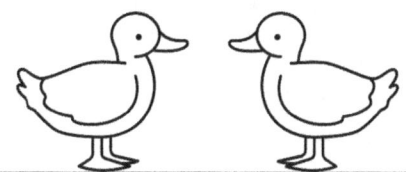

This coloring book belongs to:

....

....

....

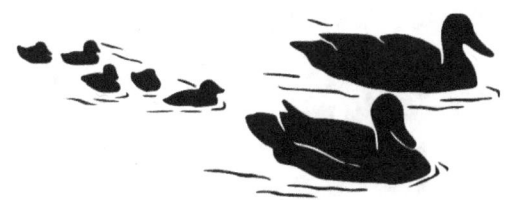

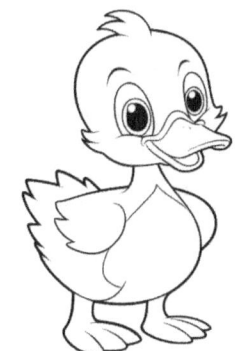

"Welcome"

"Welcome to the enchanting world of ducks! This coloring book invites you to dive into fun and creativity as you bring adorable ducks to life with your favorite colors. Let your imagination soar and enjoy hours of joy exploring the magical realm of these cute ducks. Get ready for a unique coloring adventure, specially designed for young artists like you!"

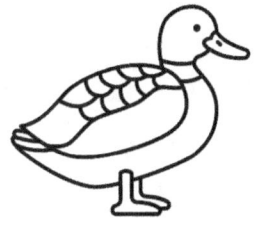

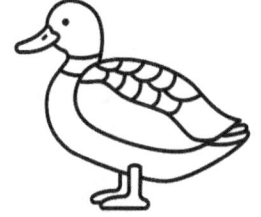

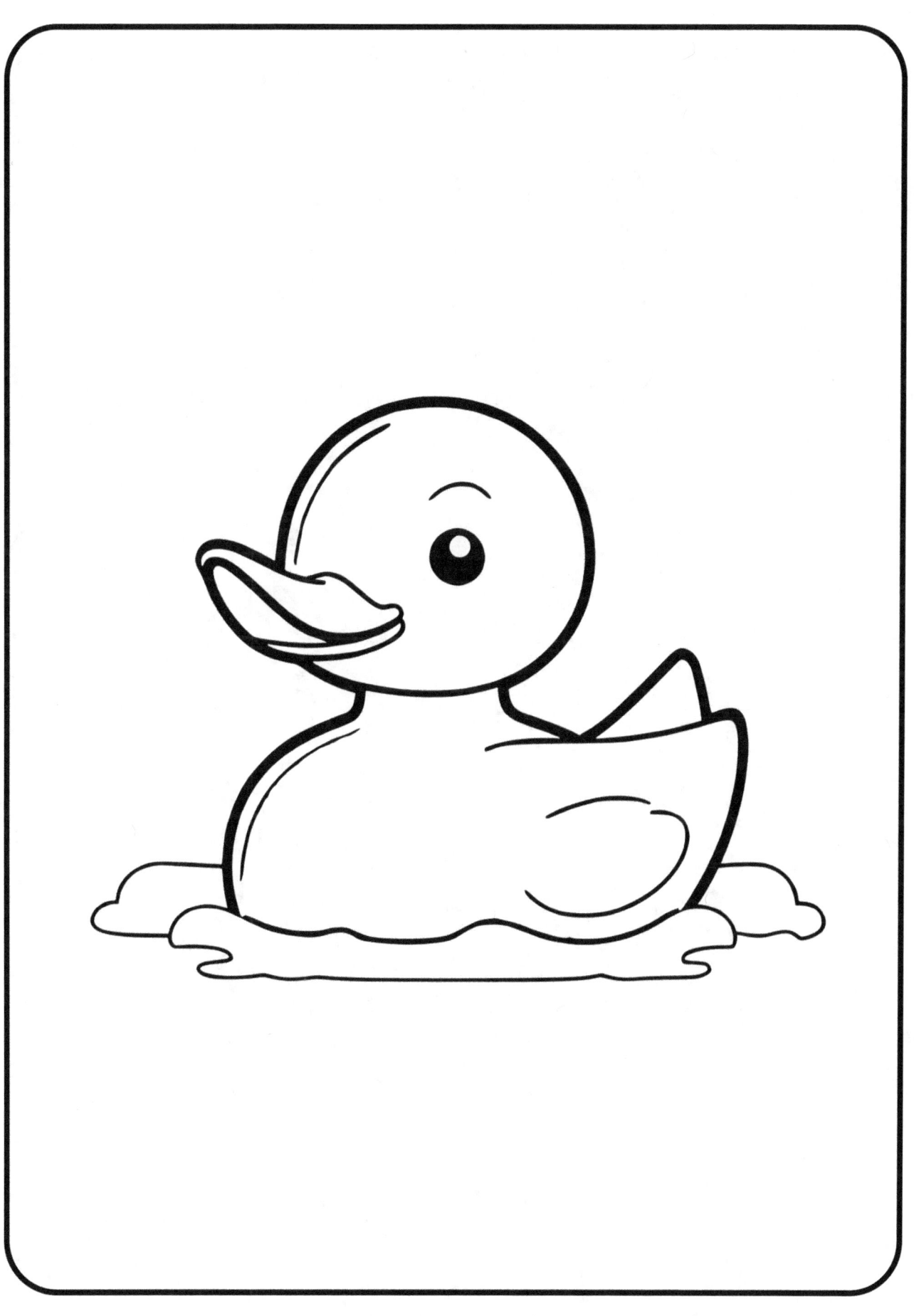

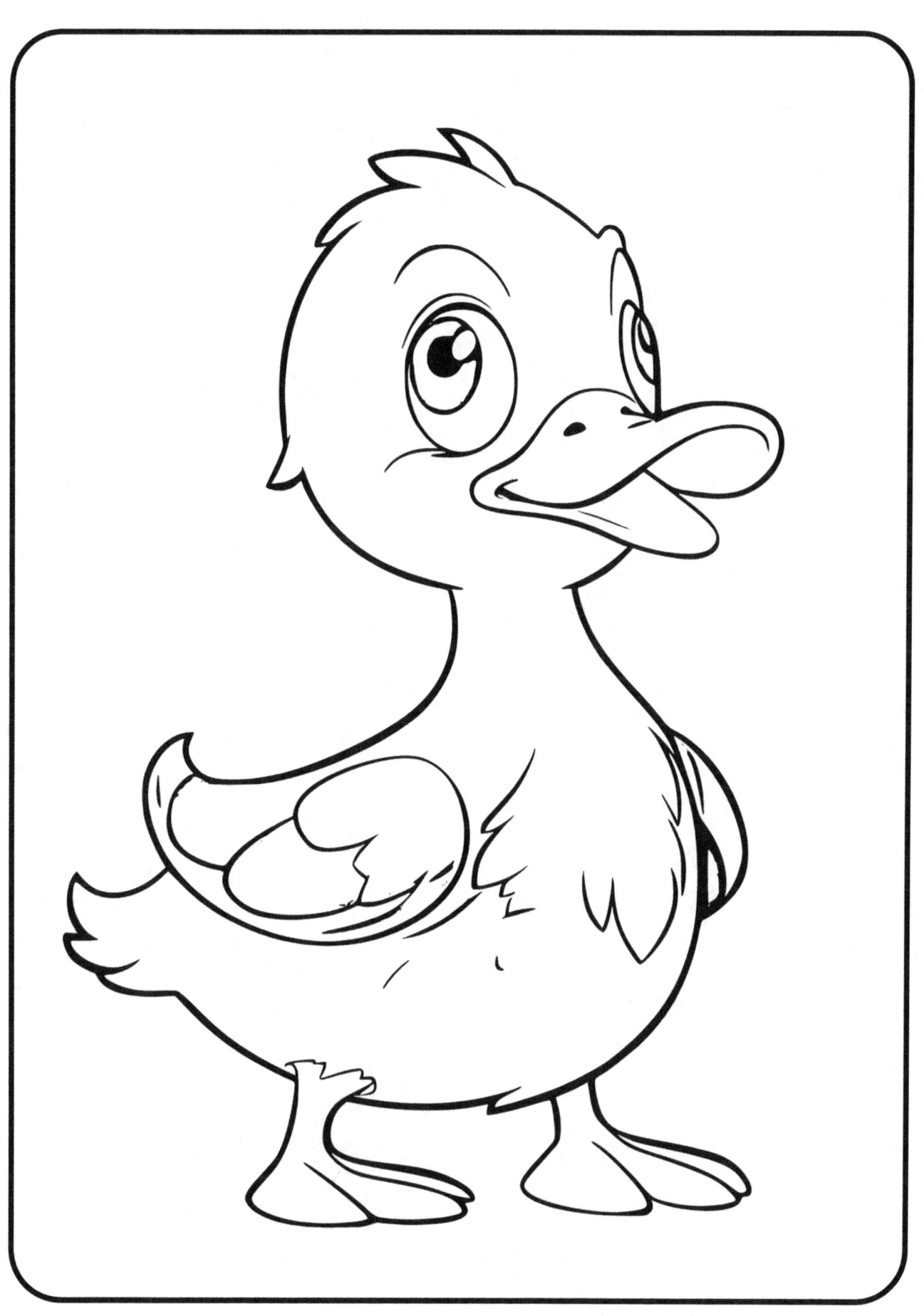

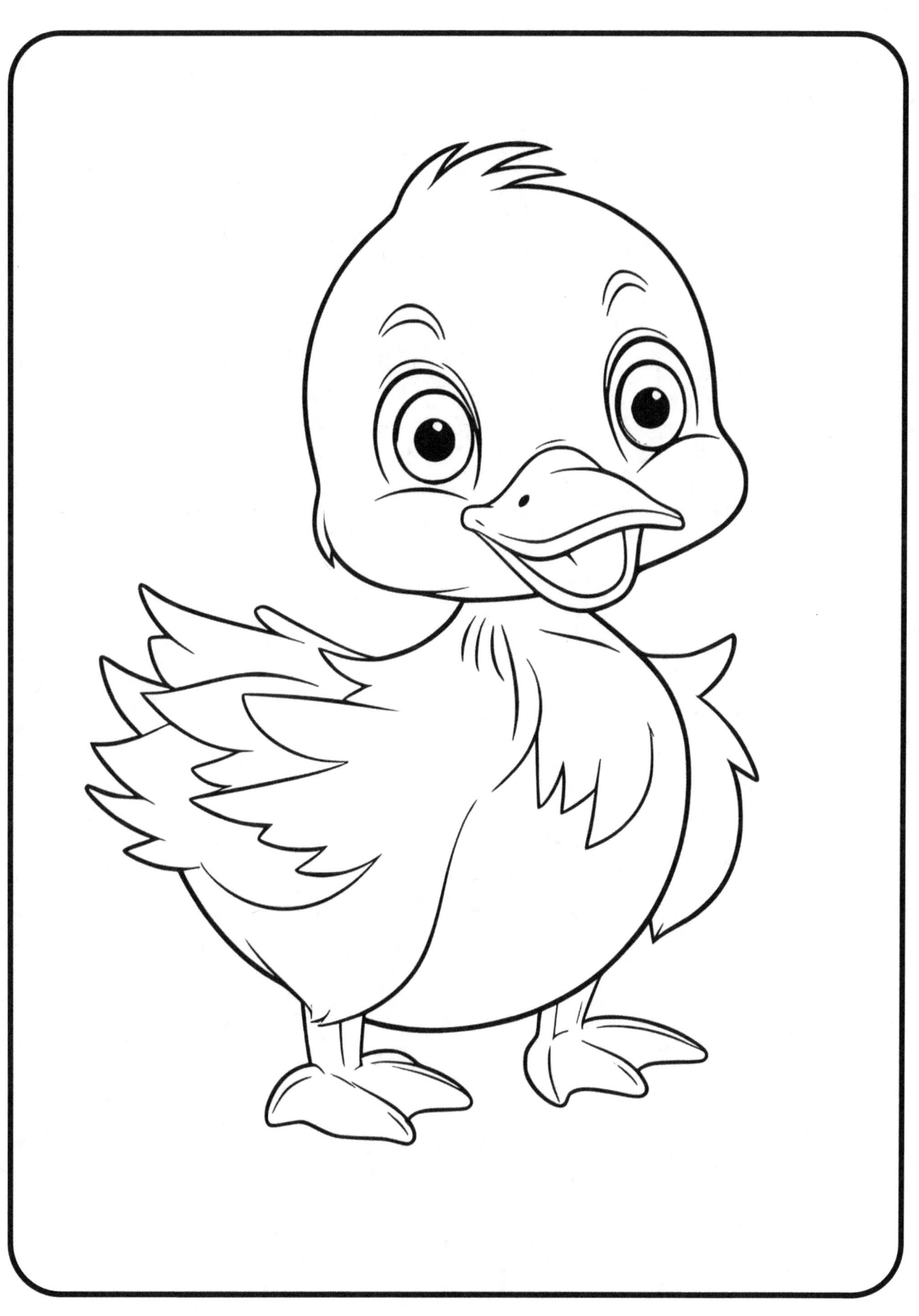

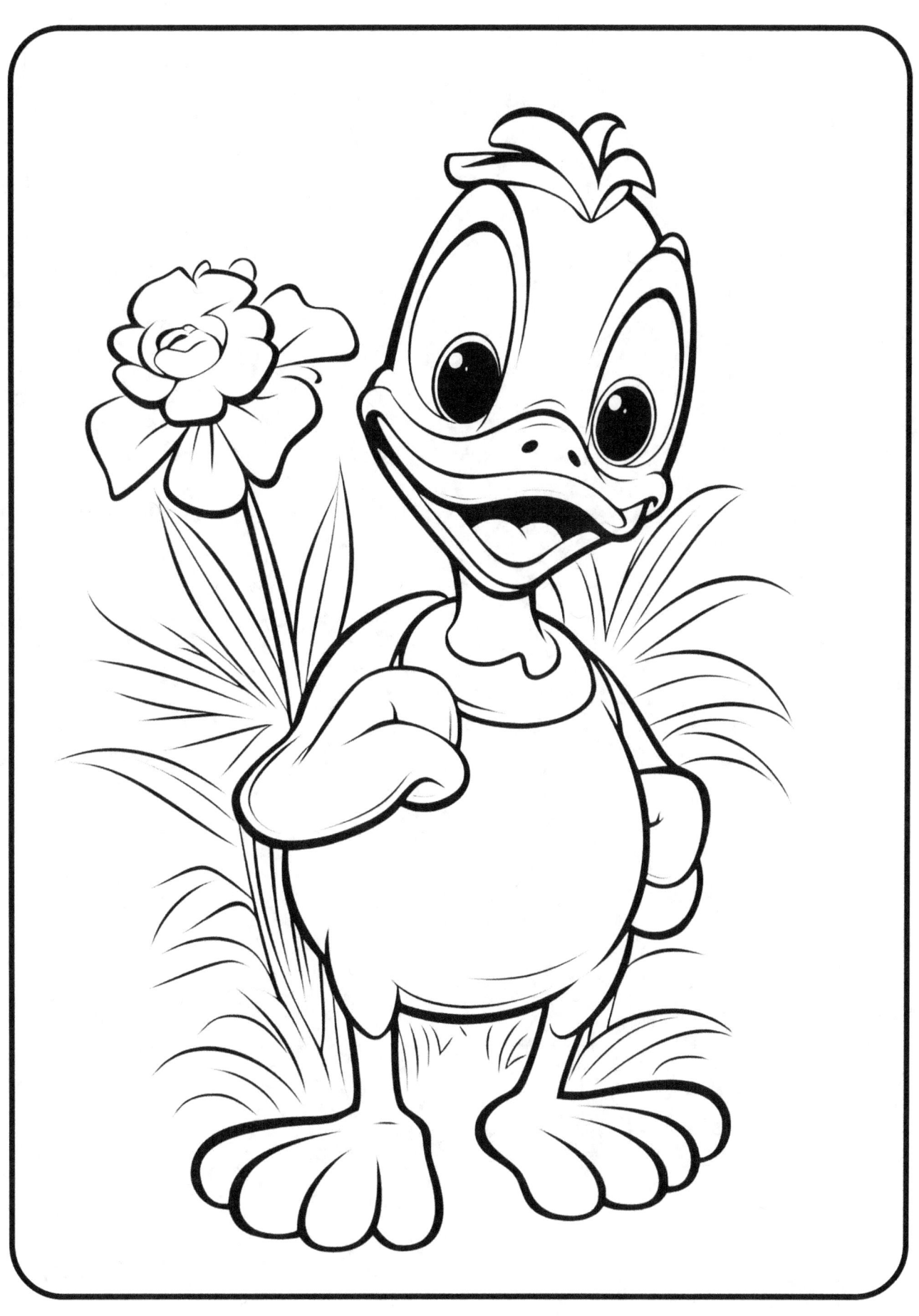

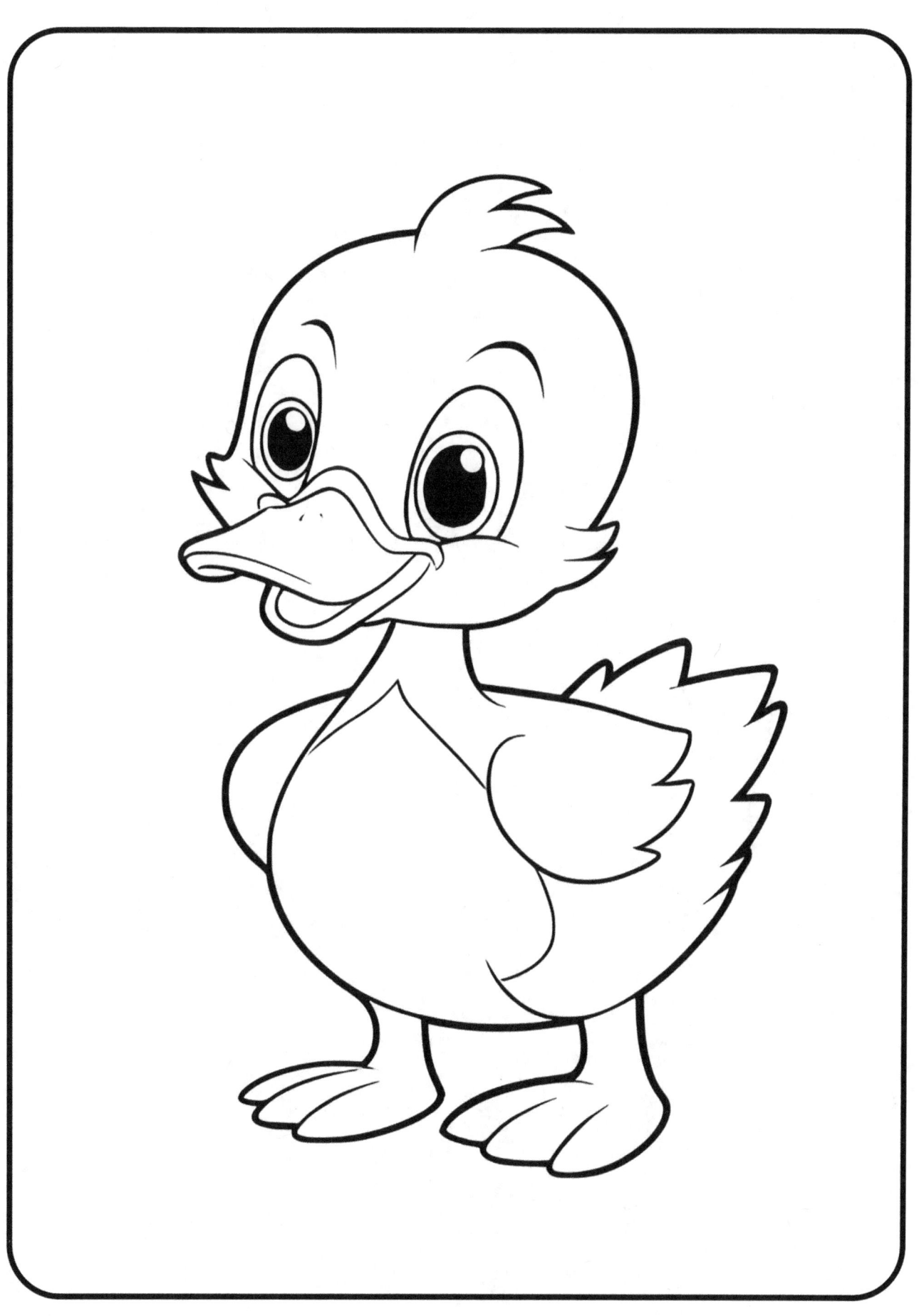

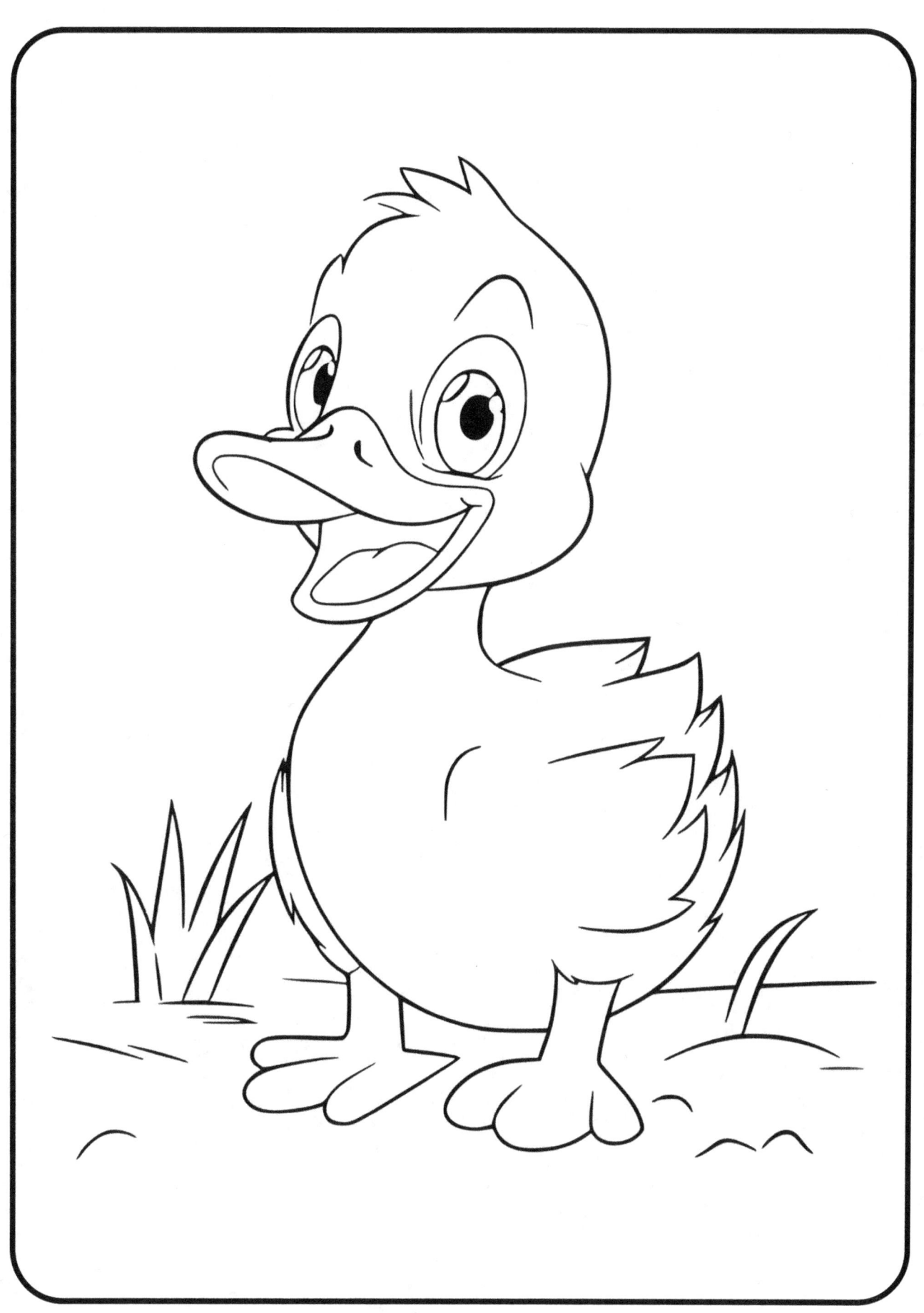

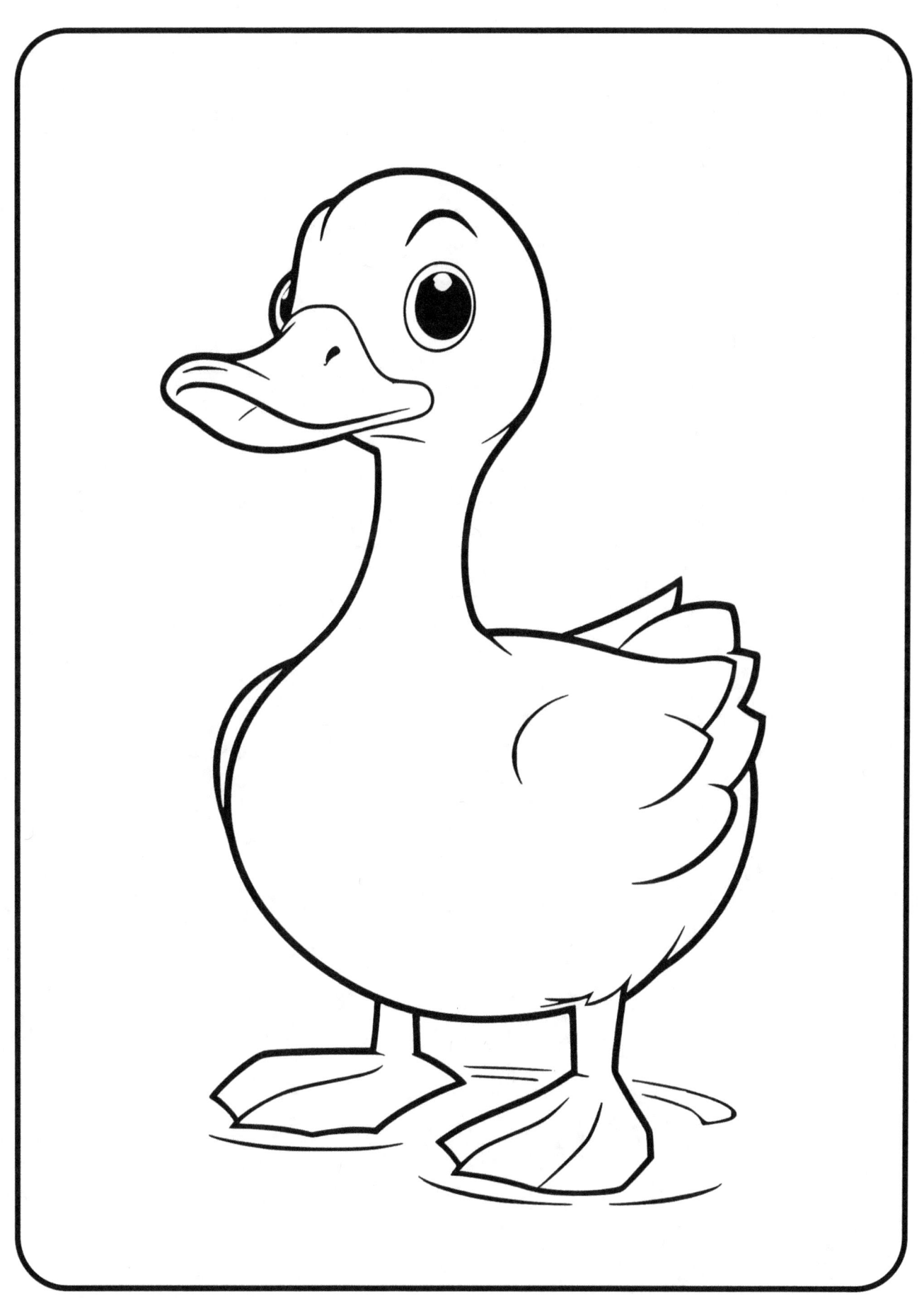

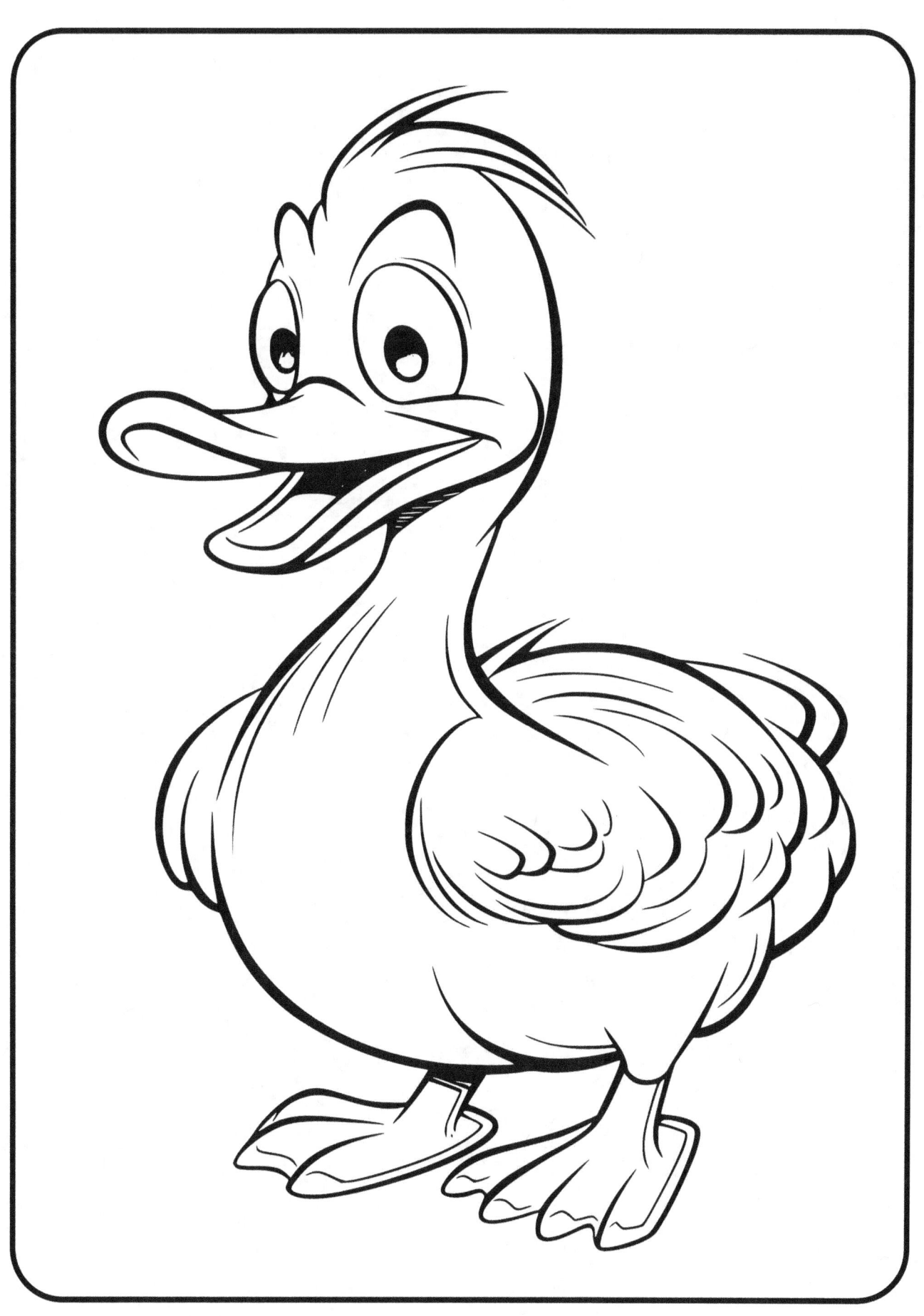

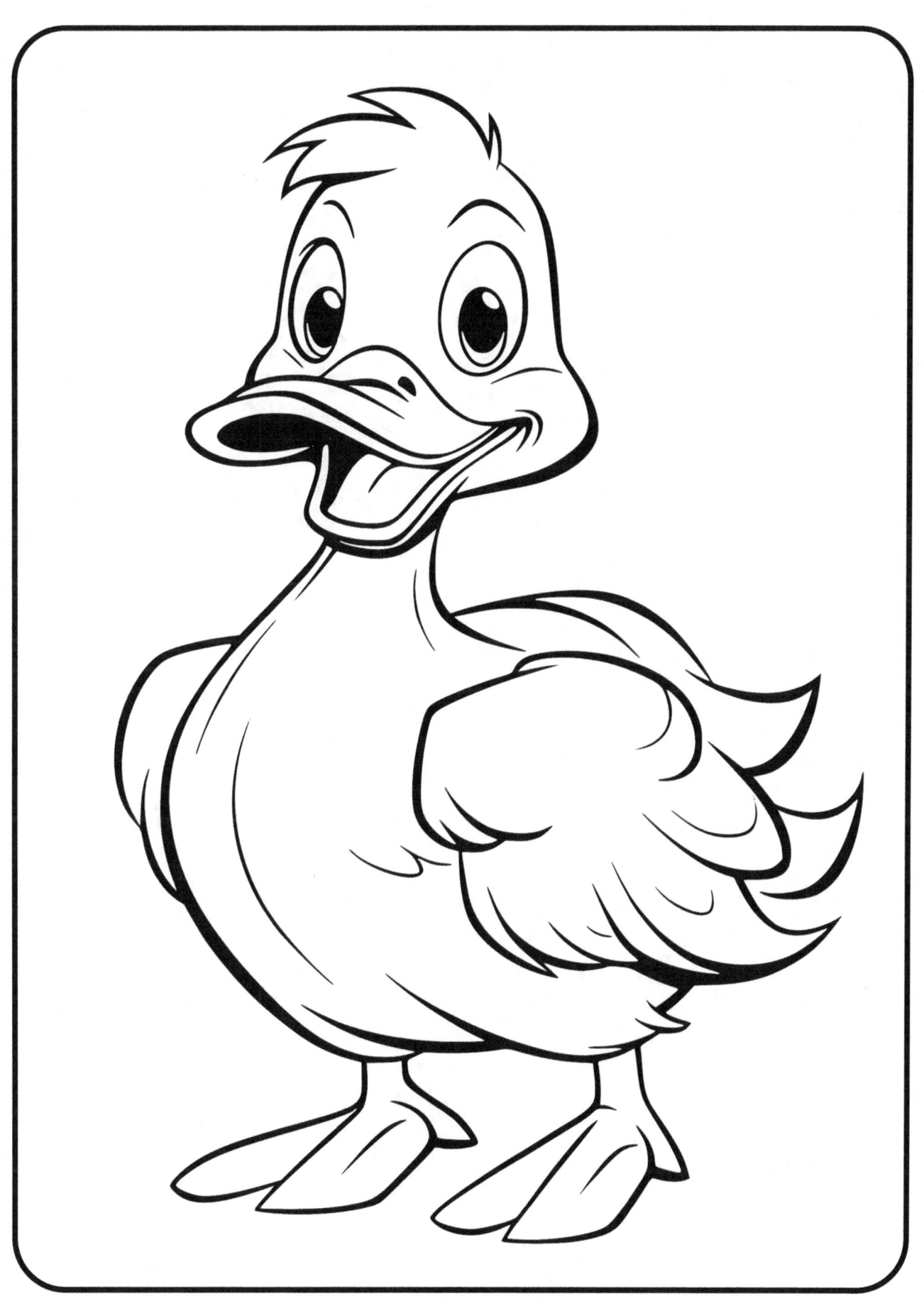

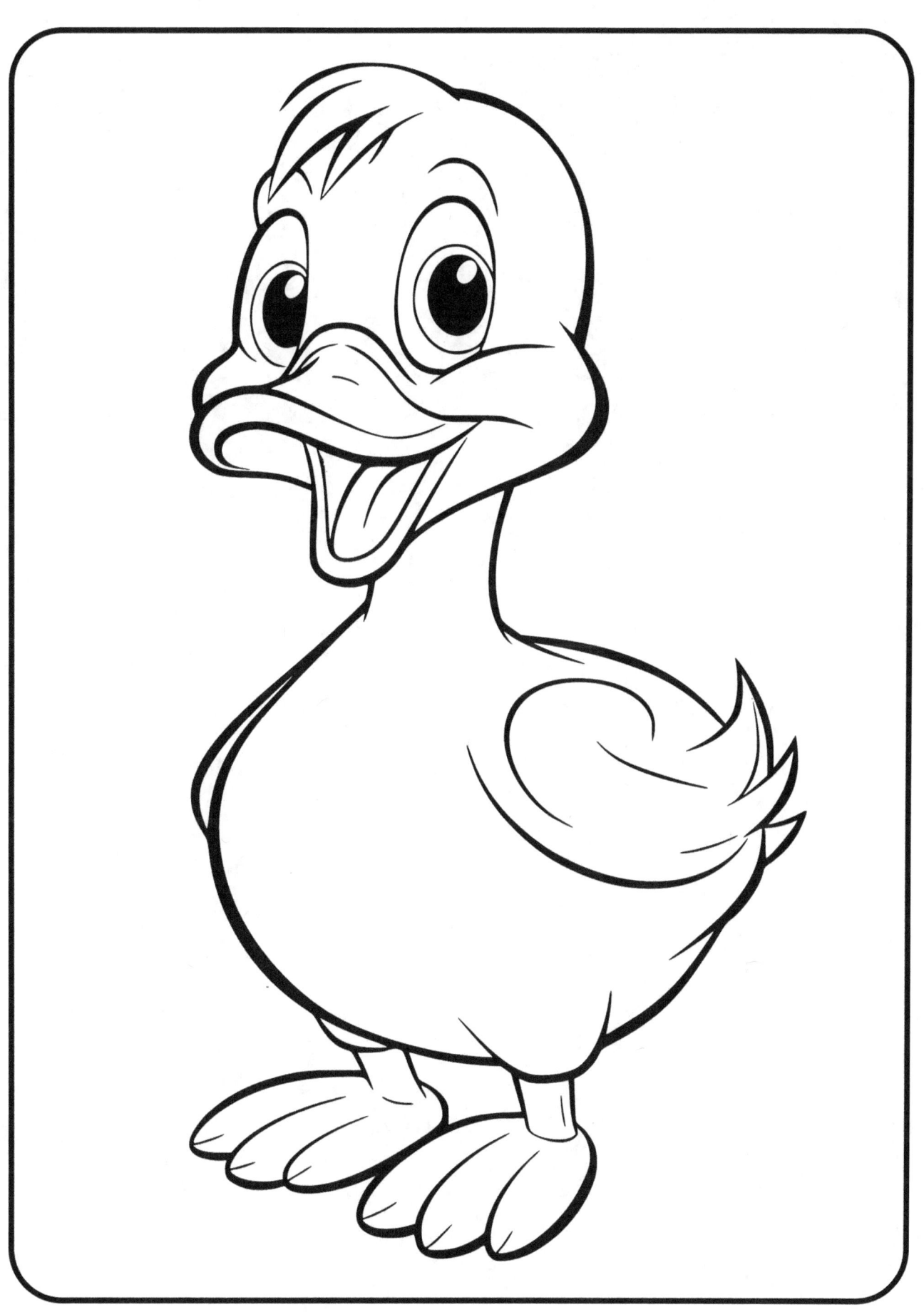

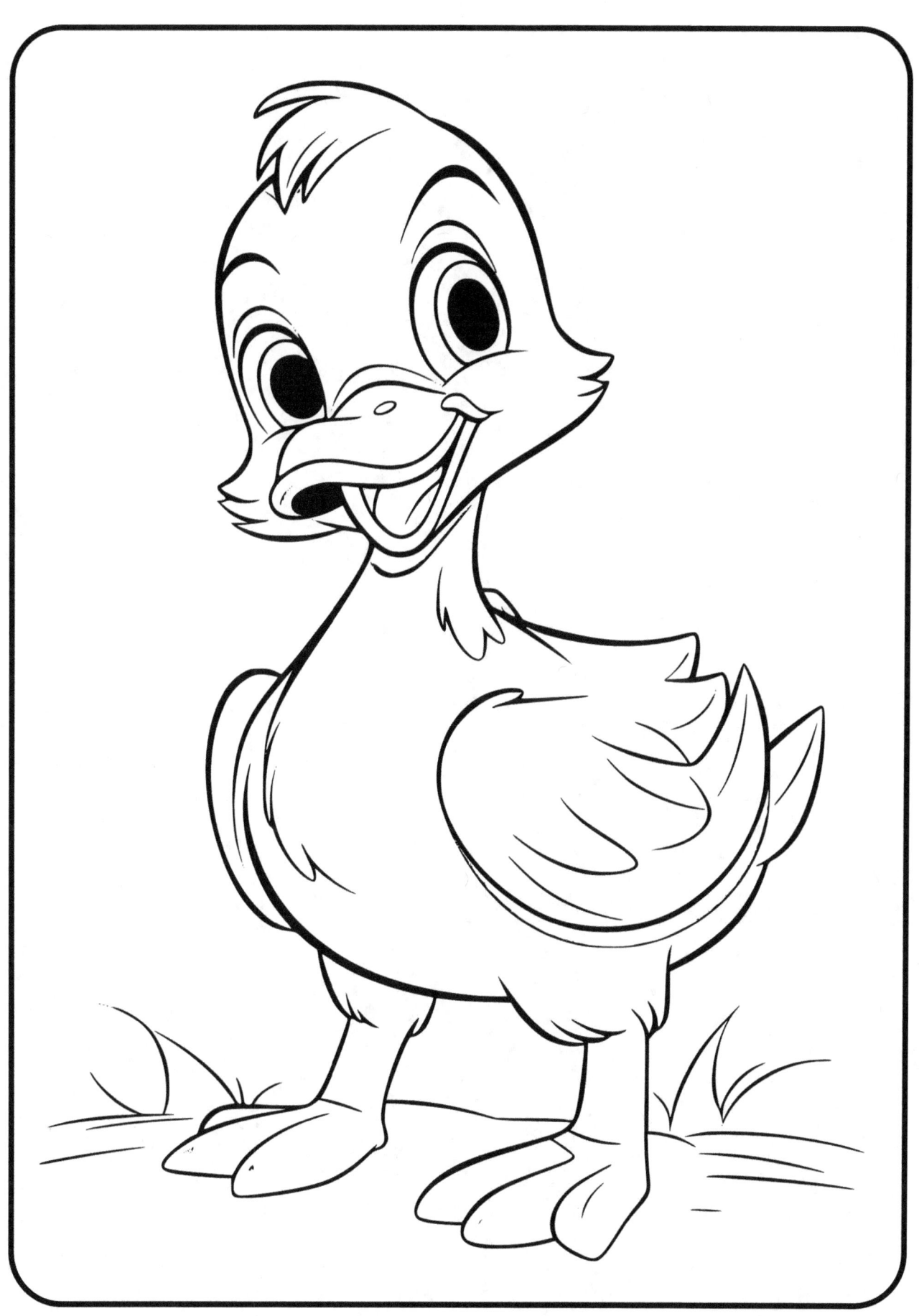

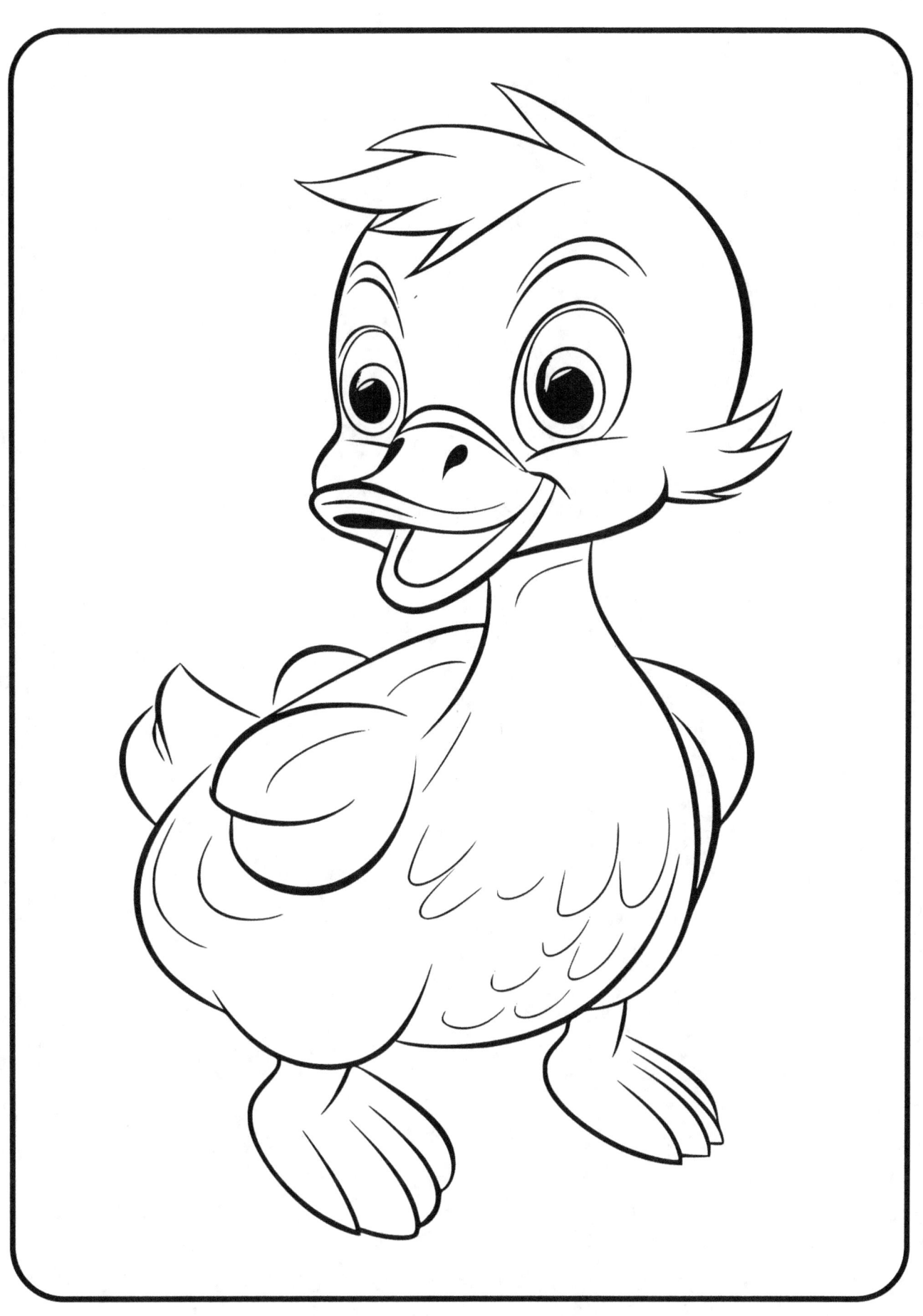

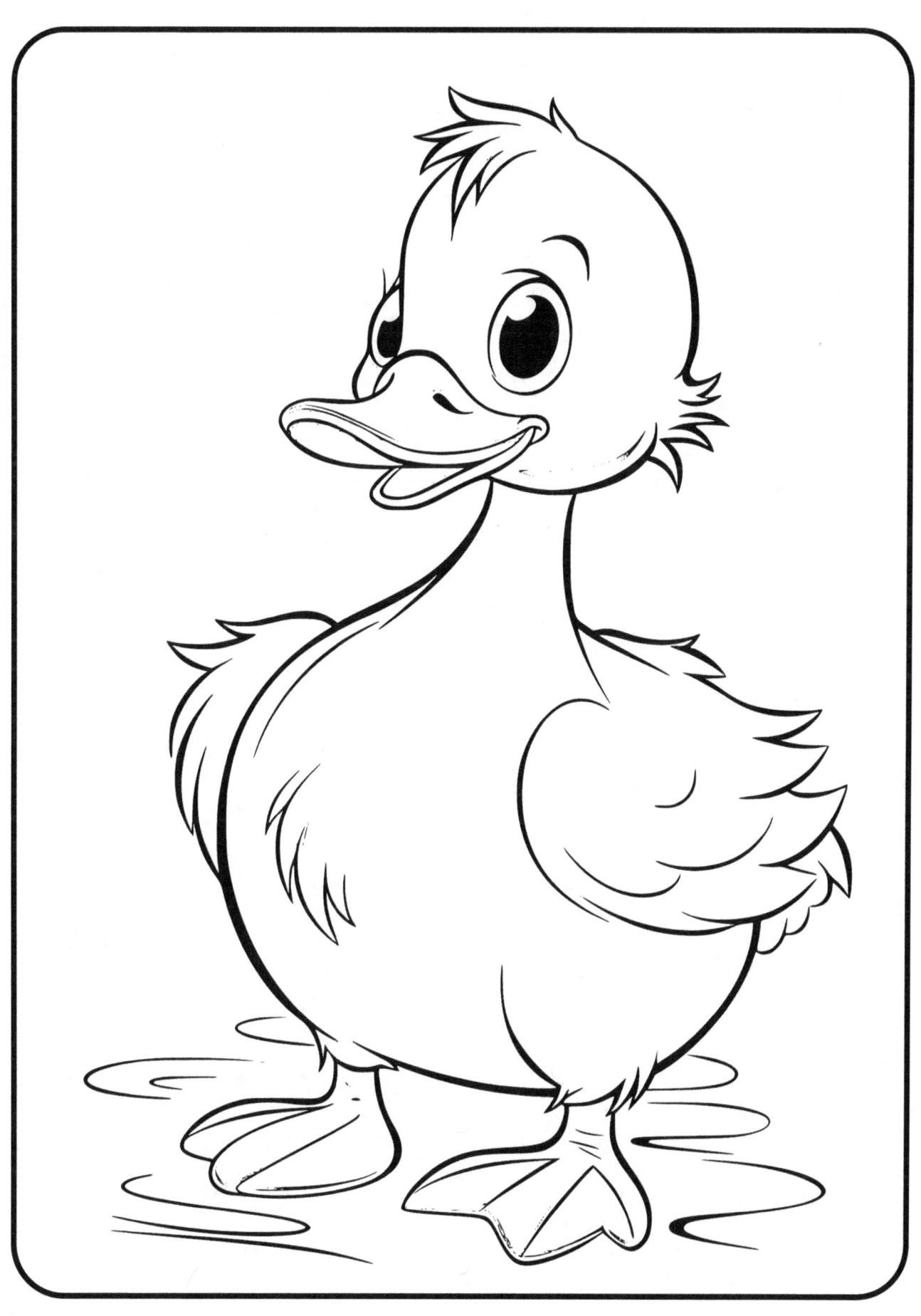

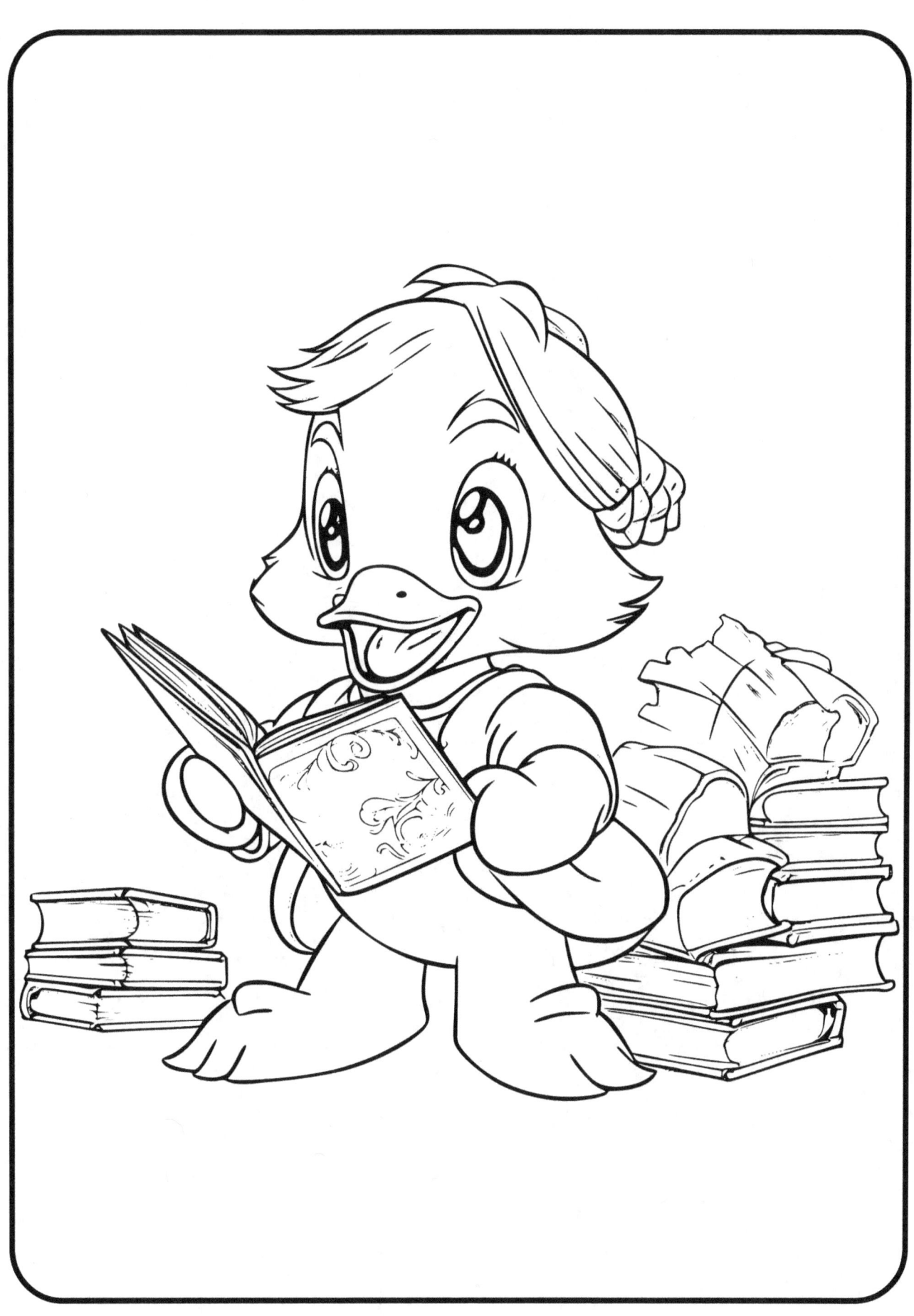

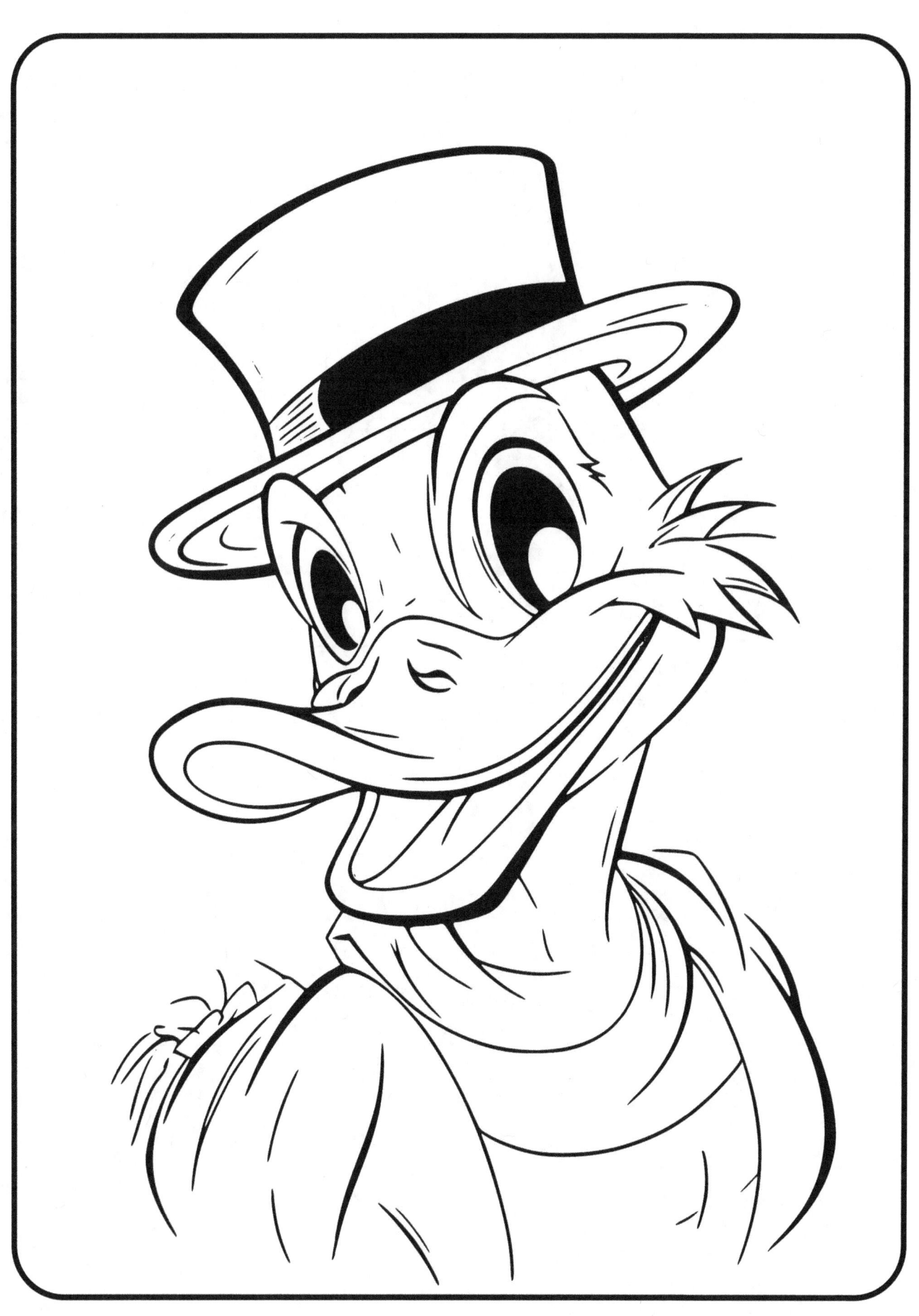

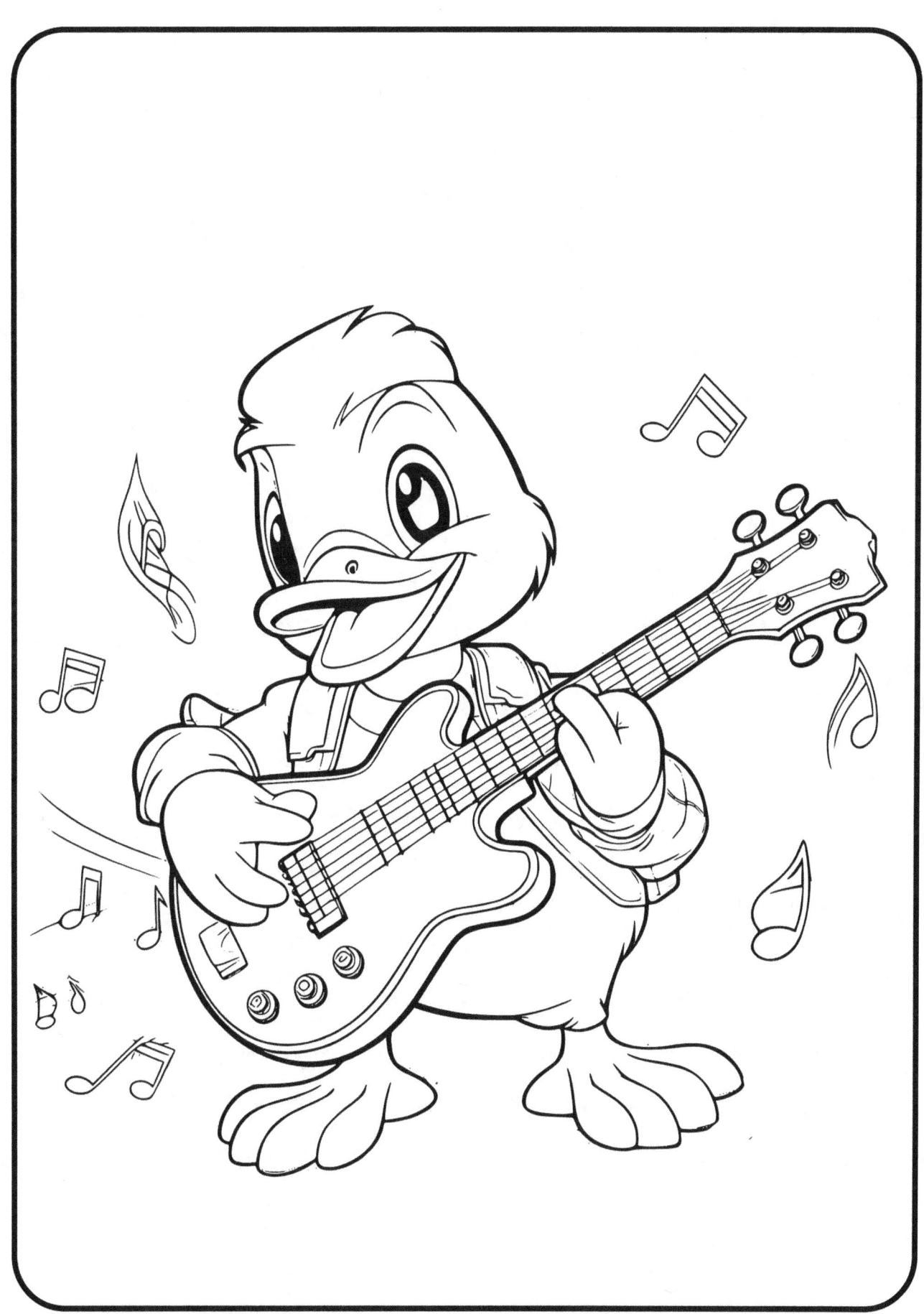

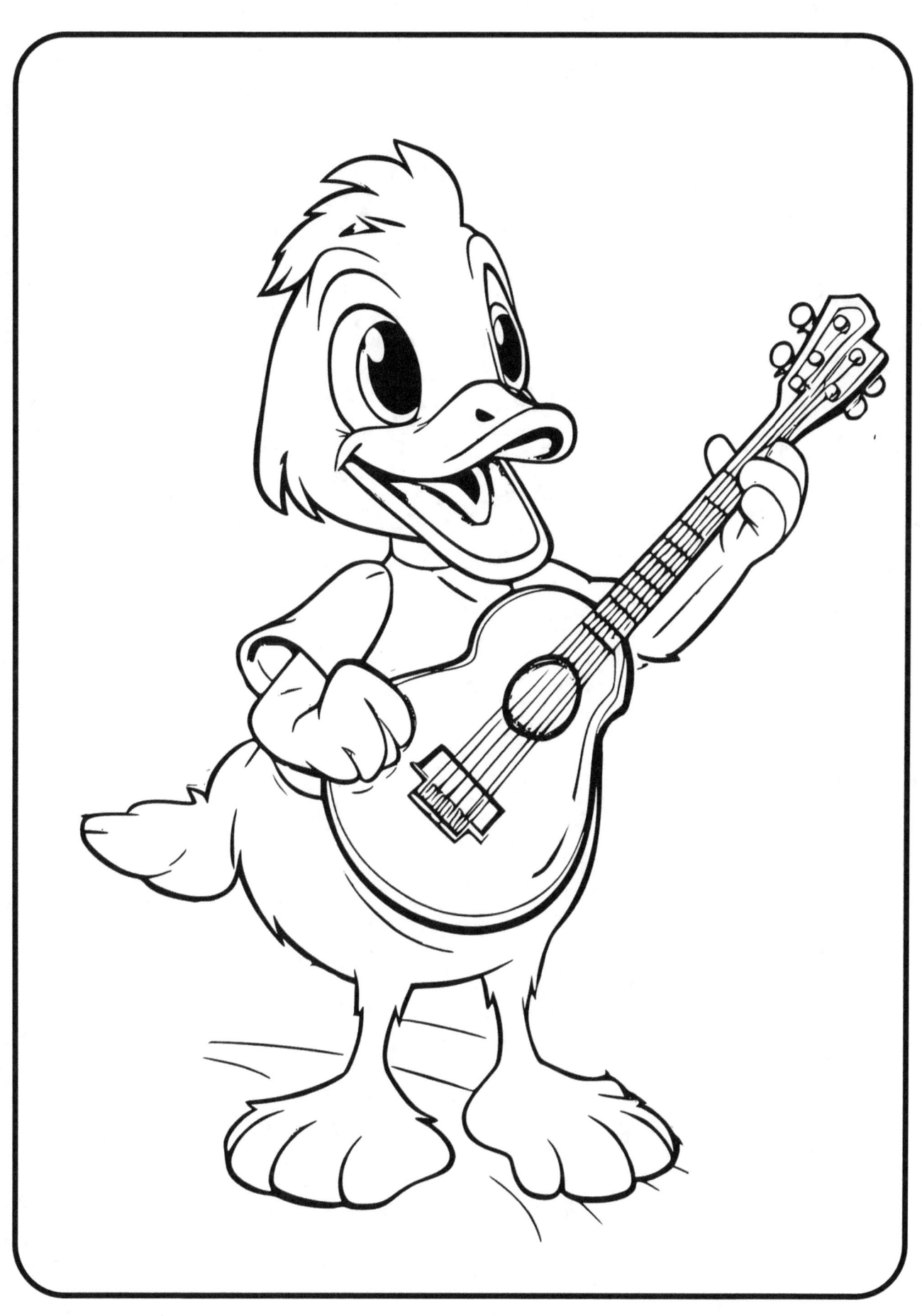

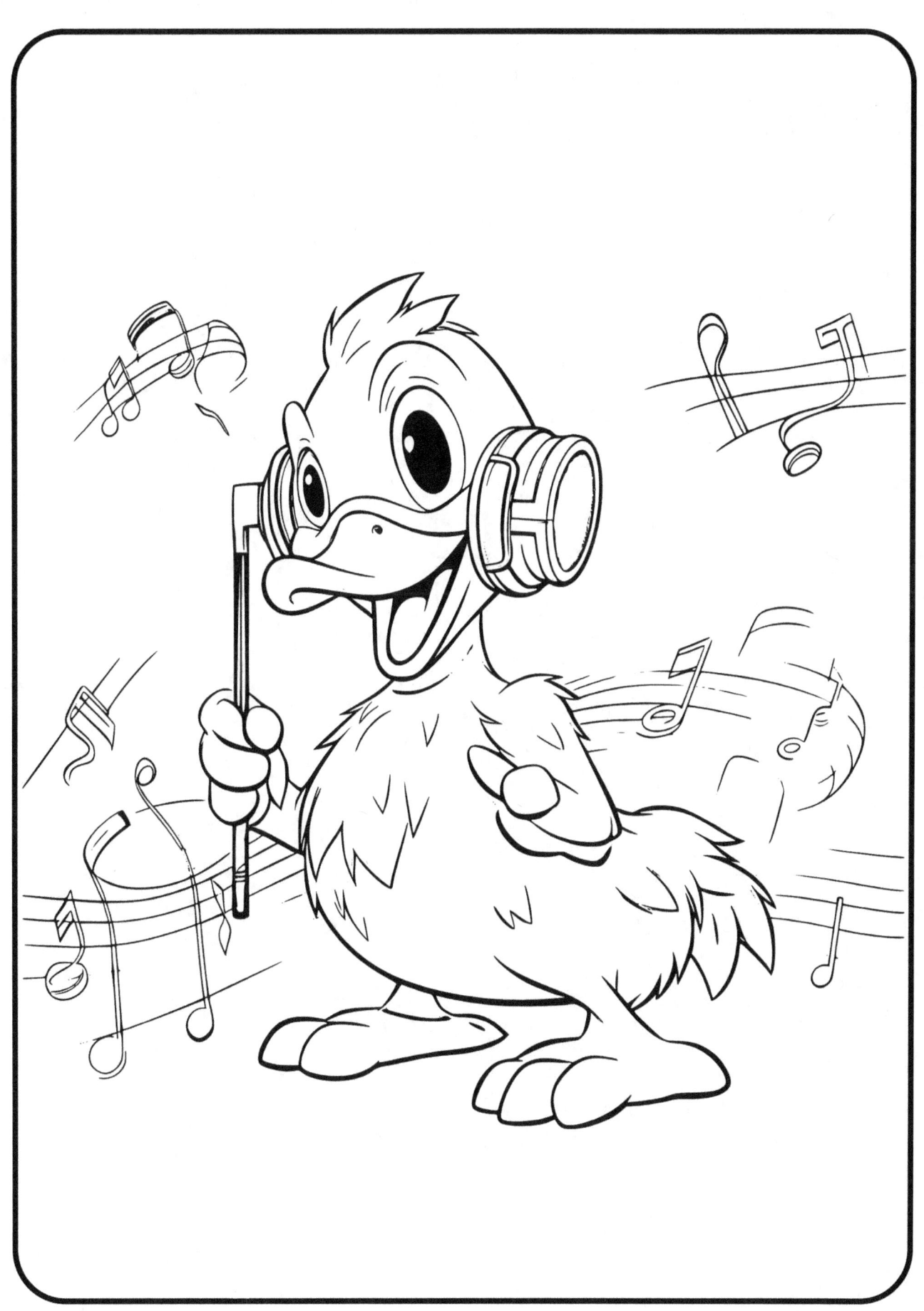

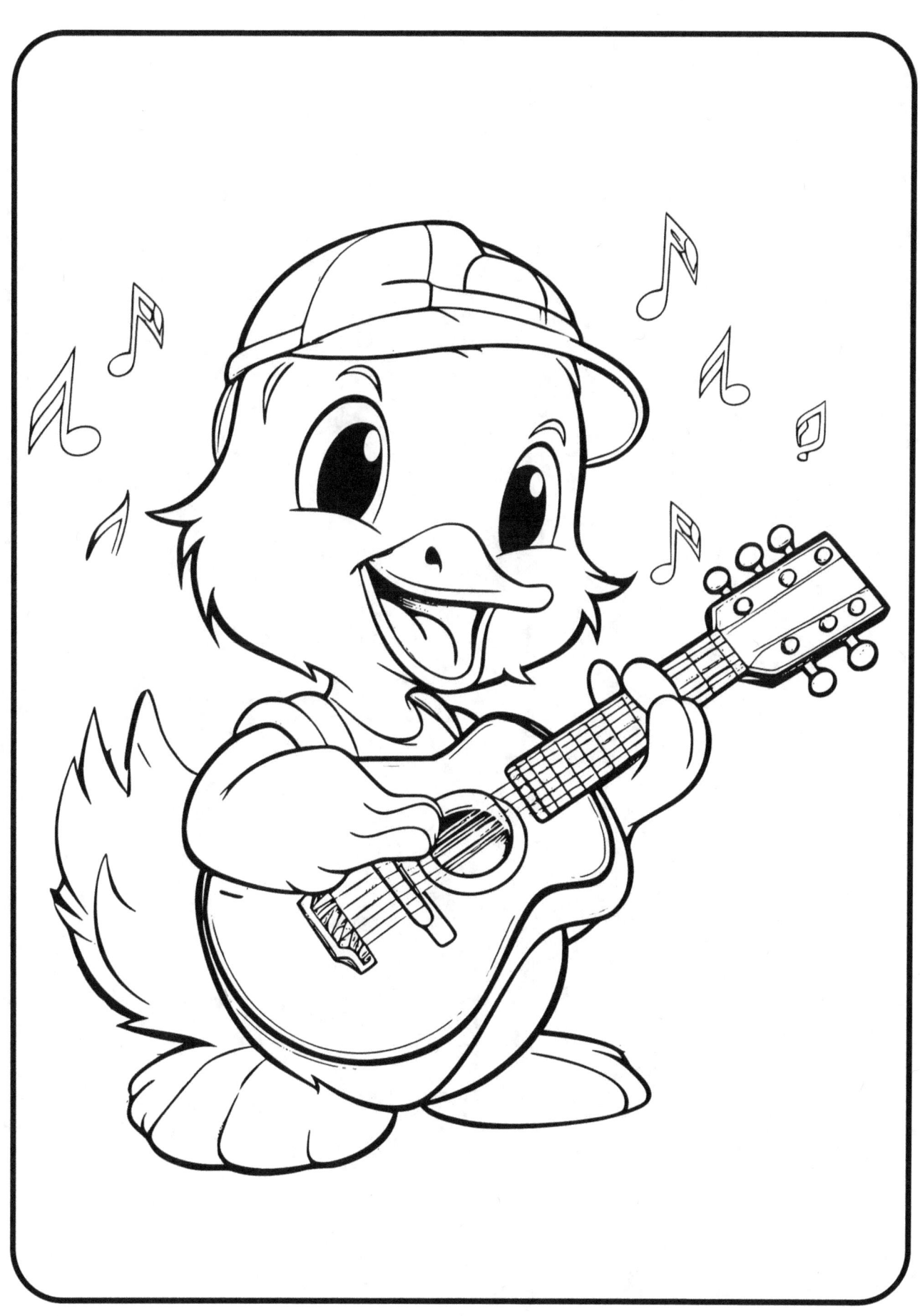

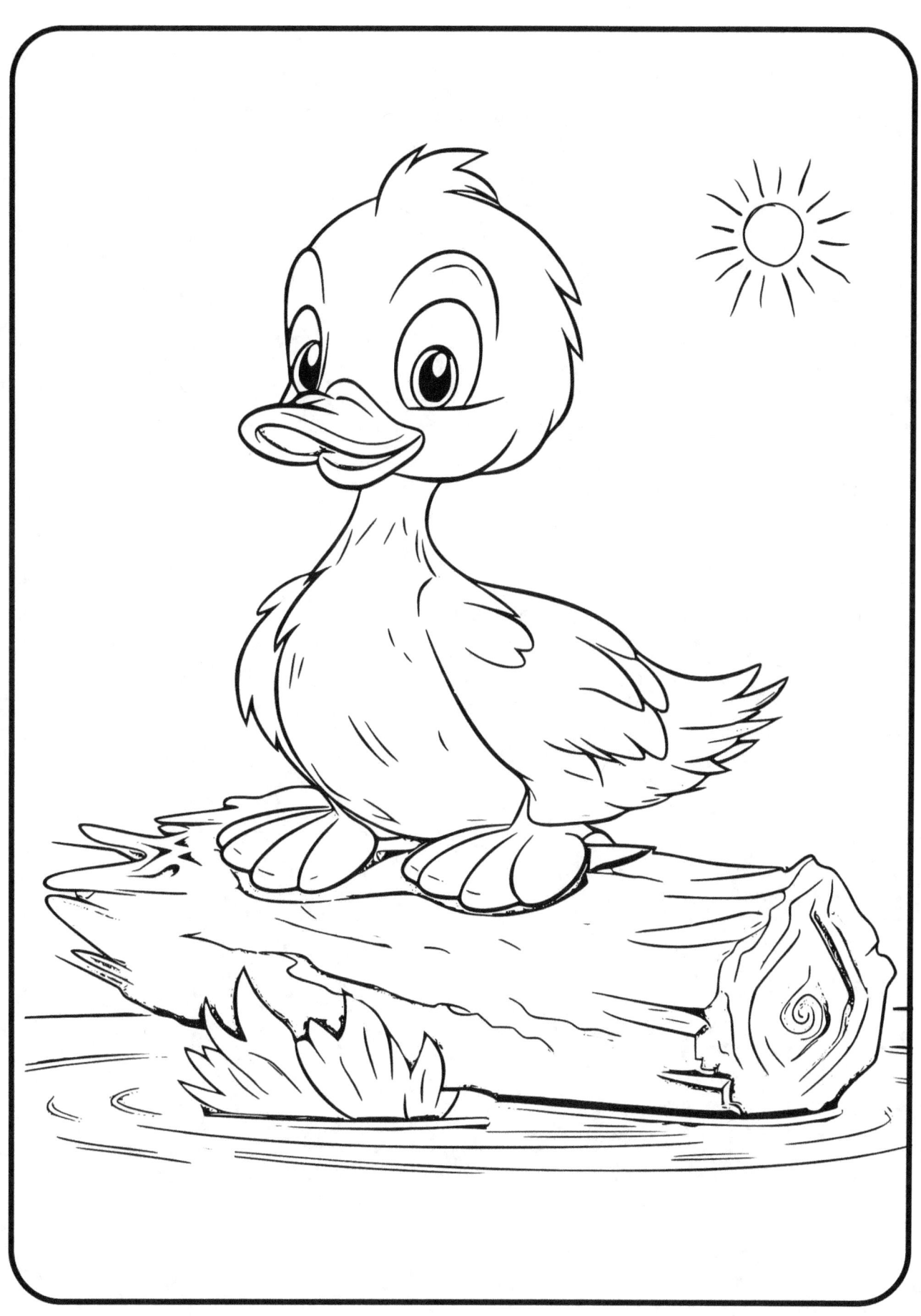

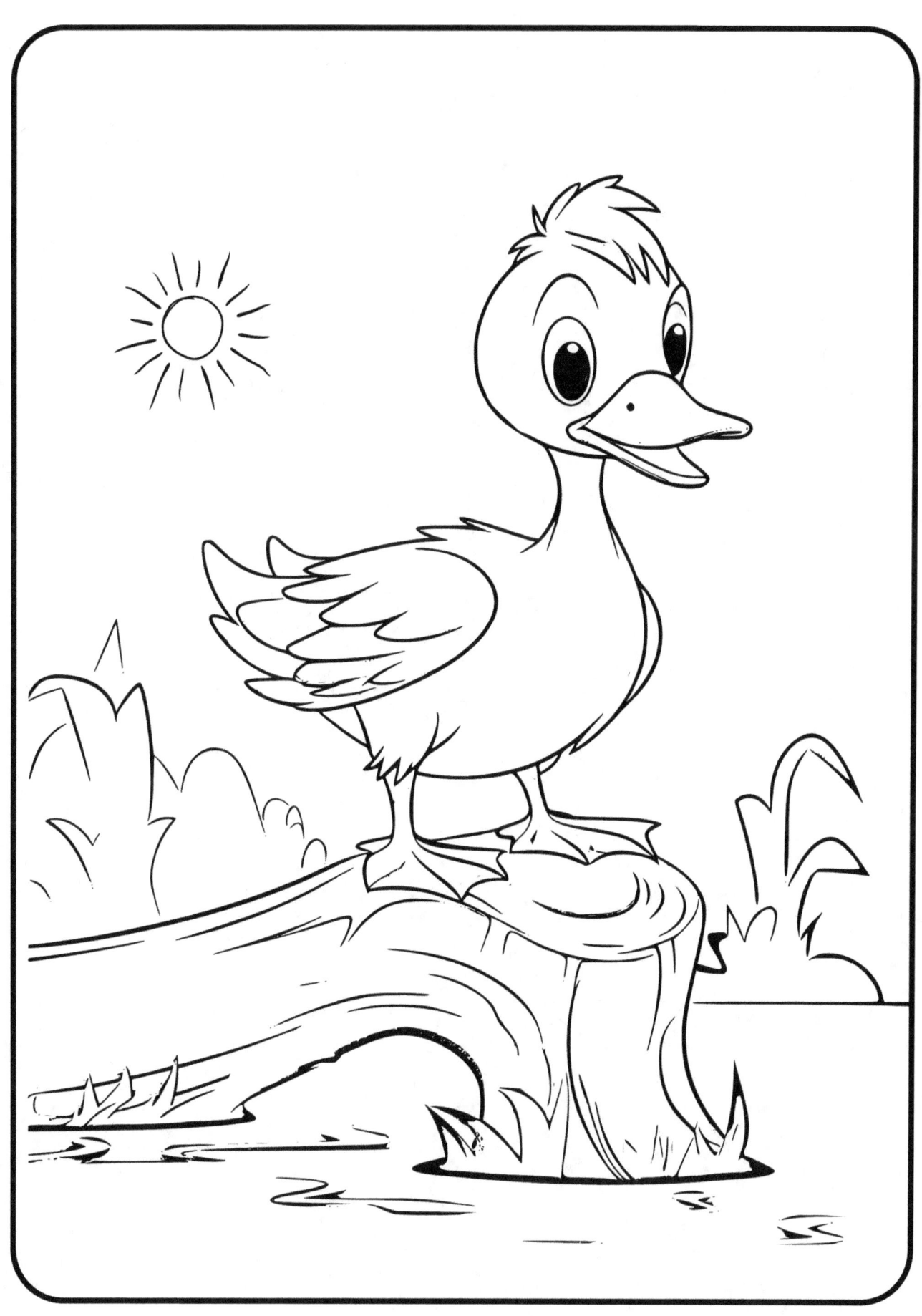

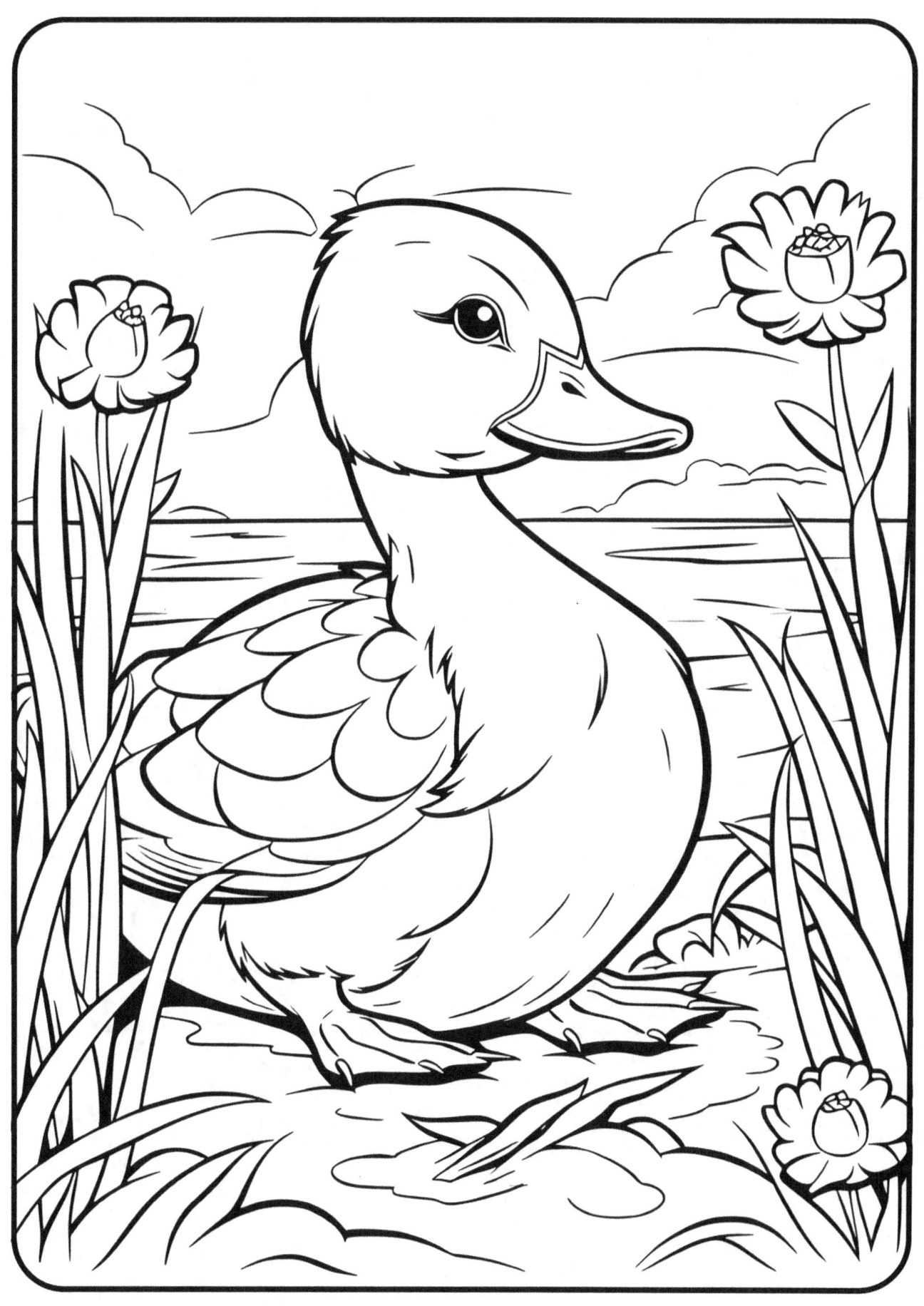

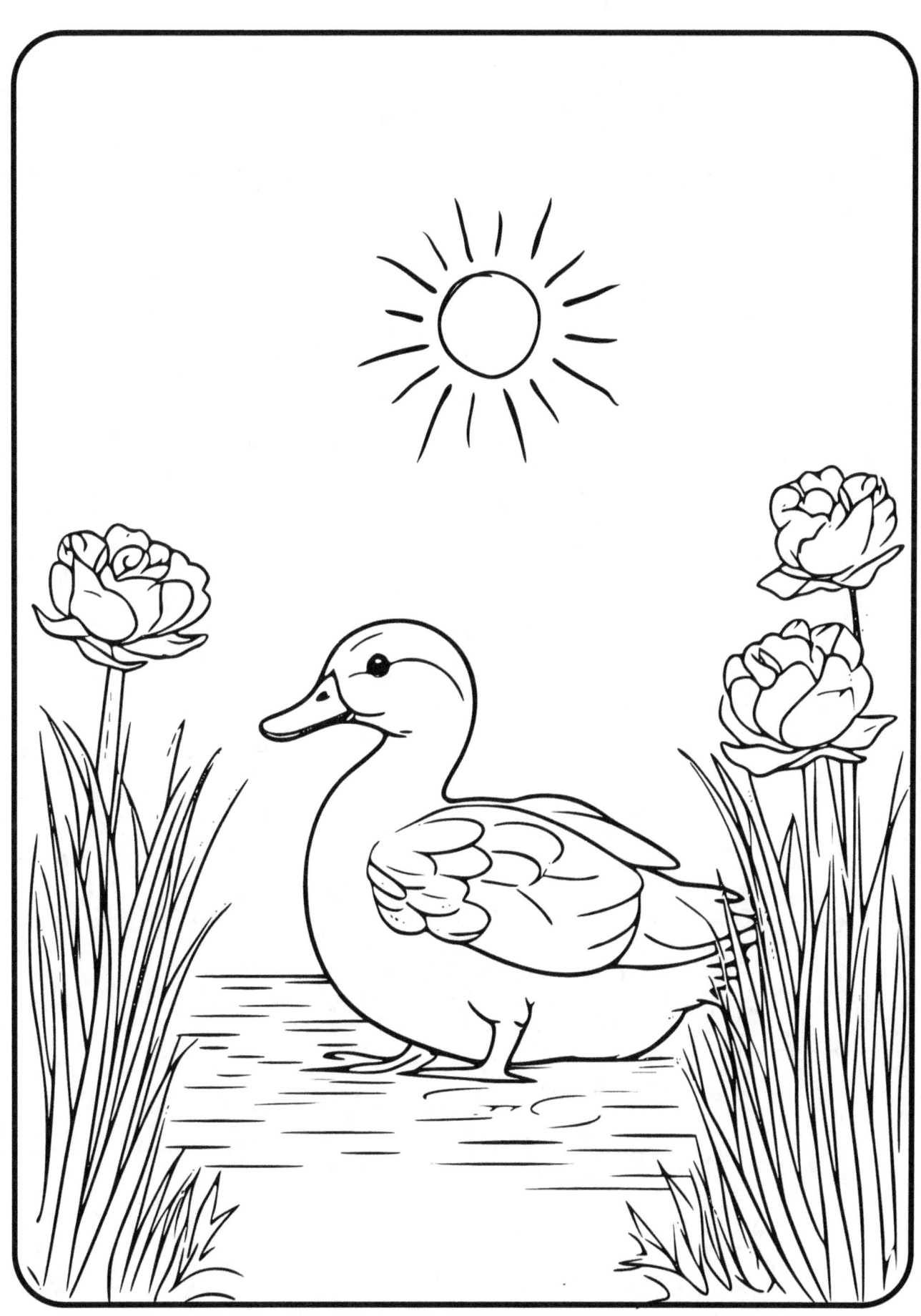

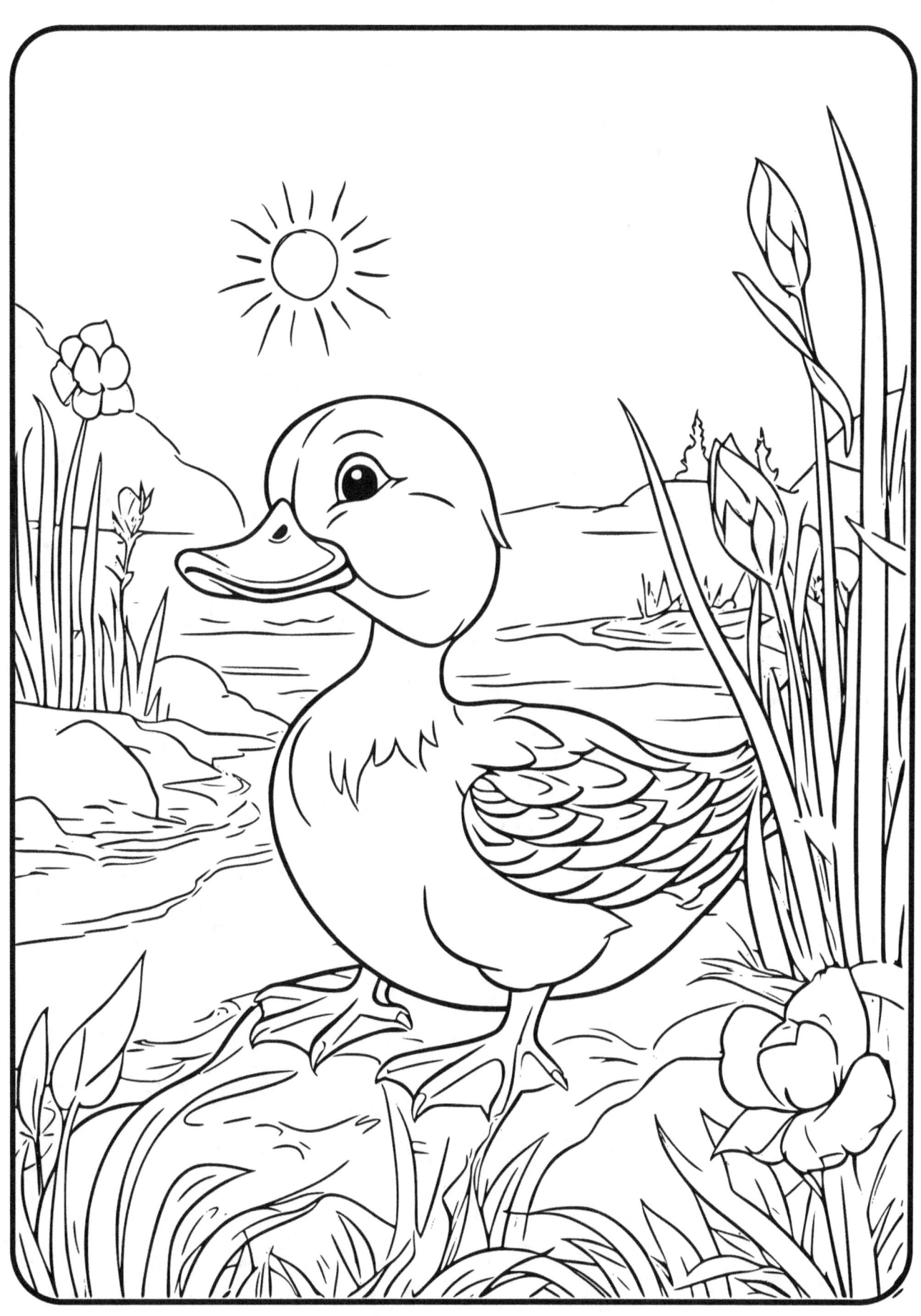

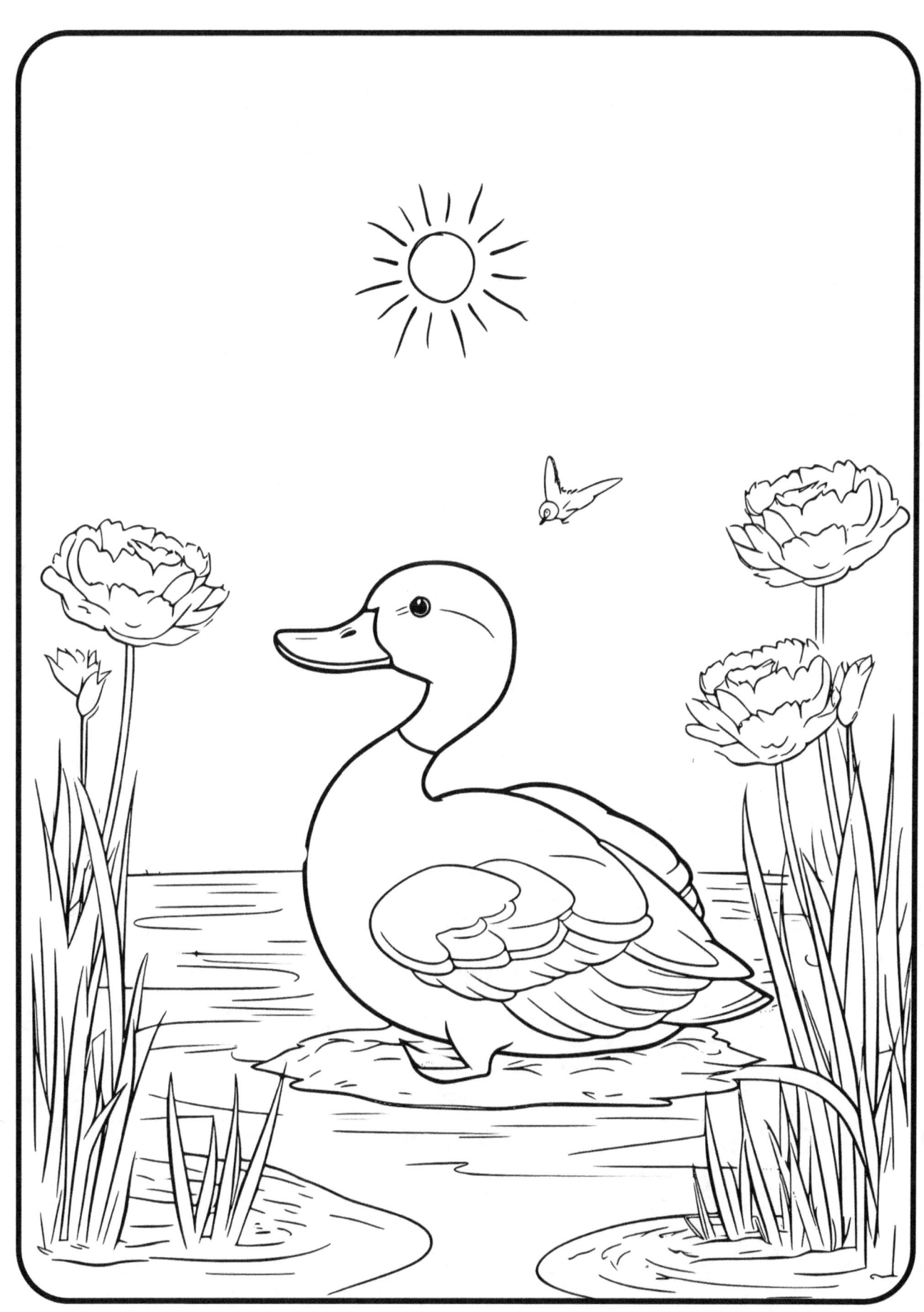

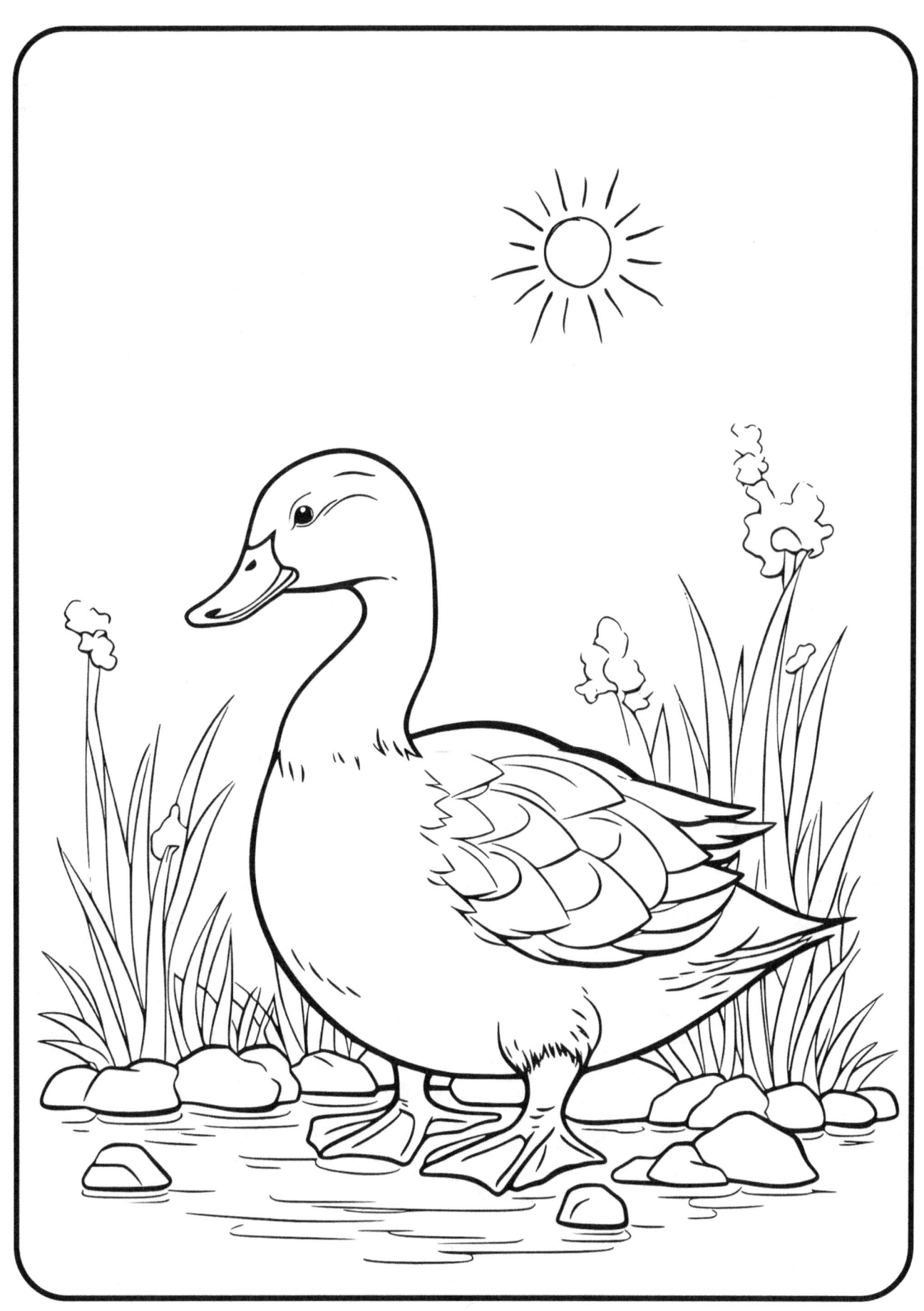

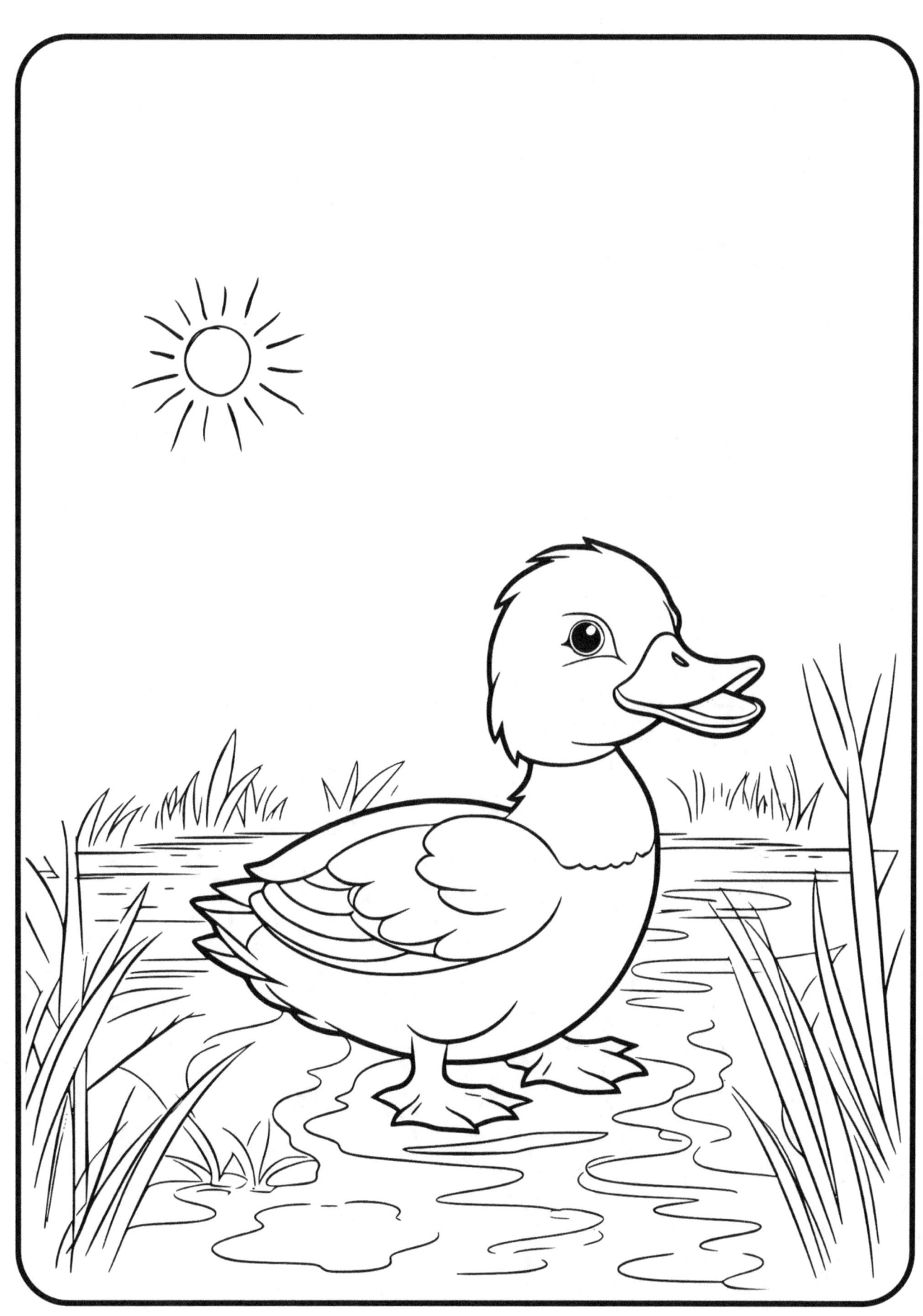

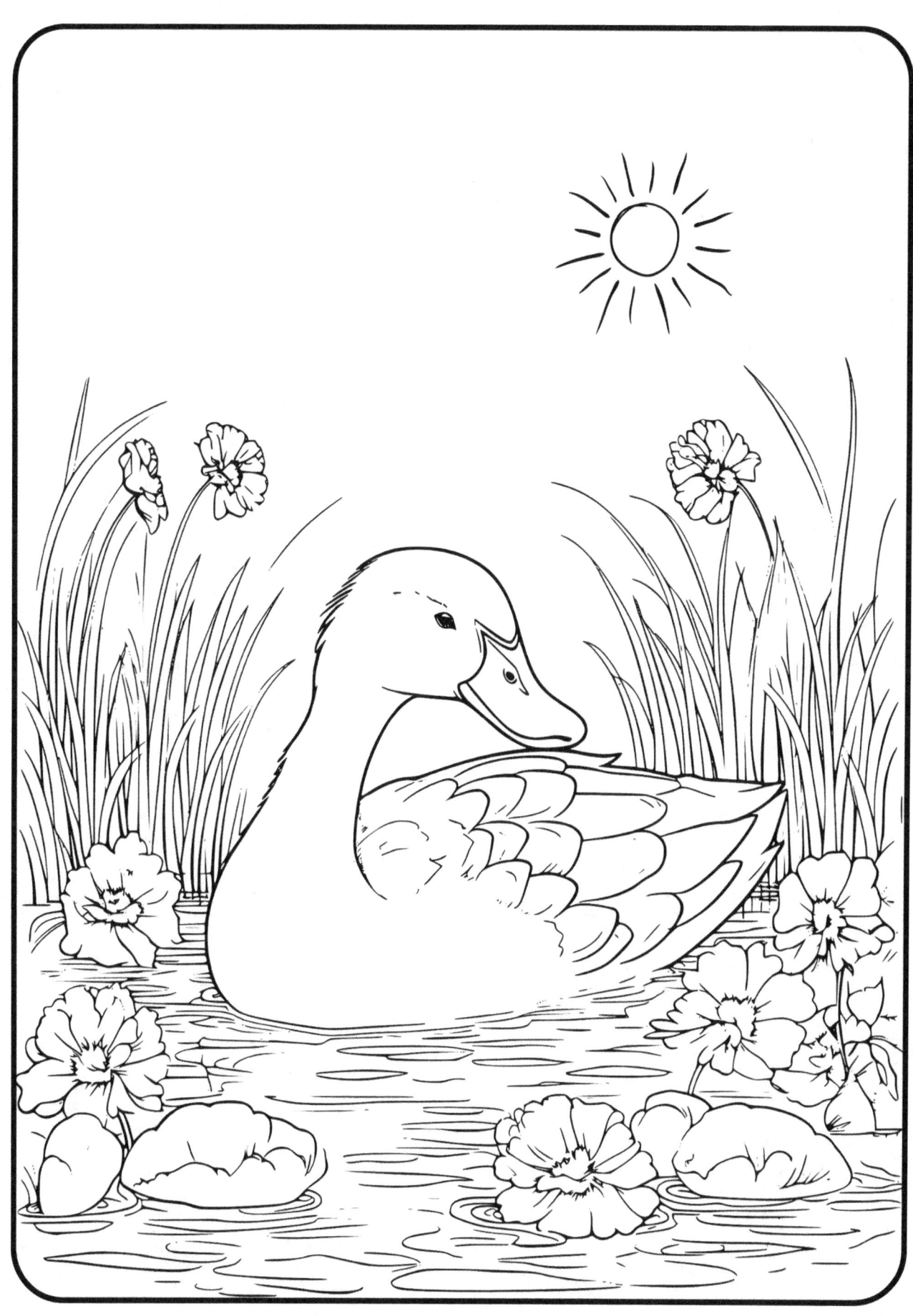

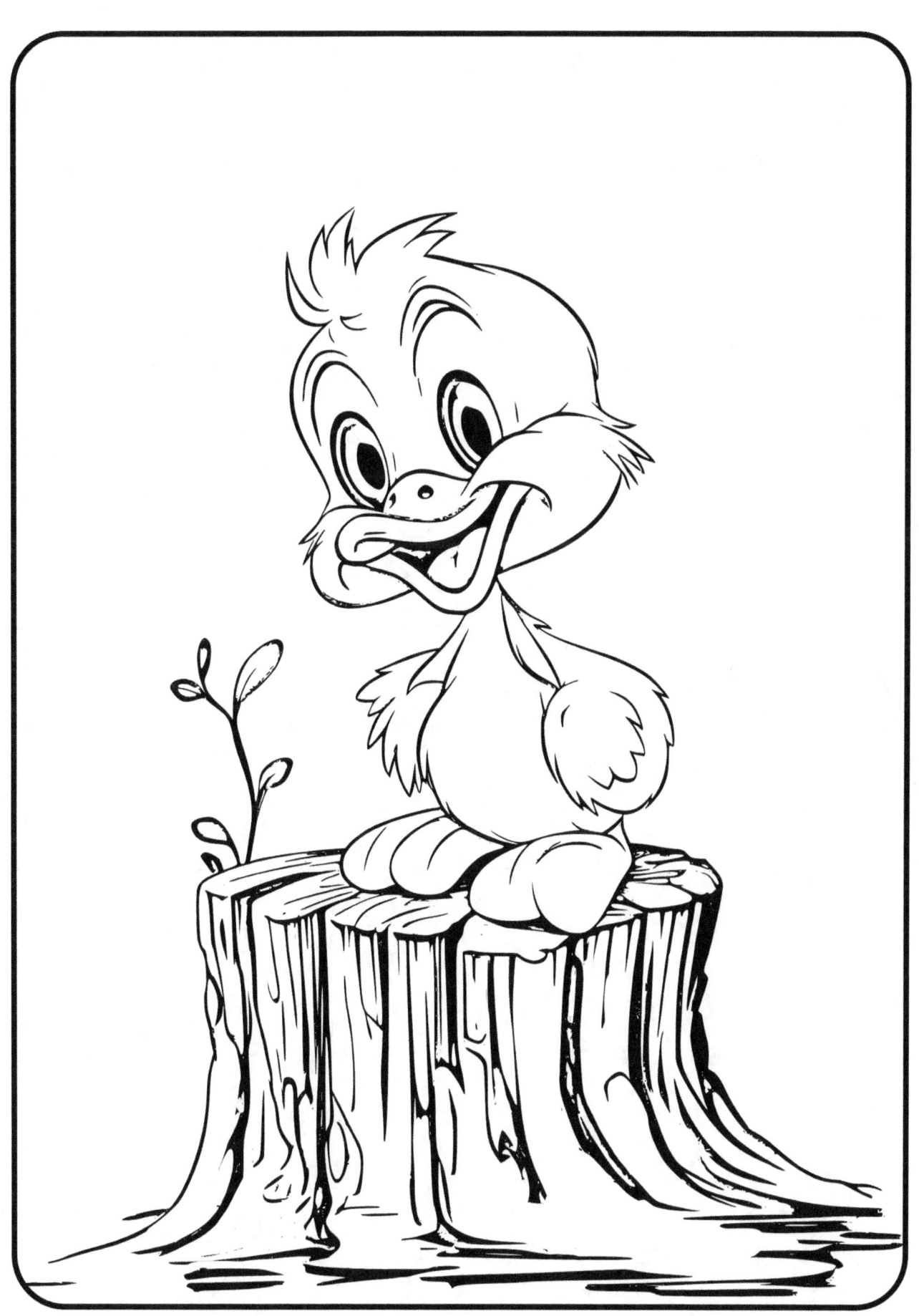

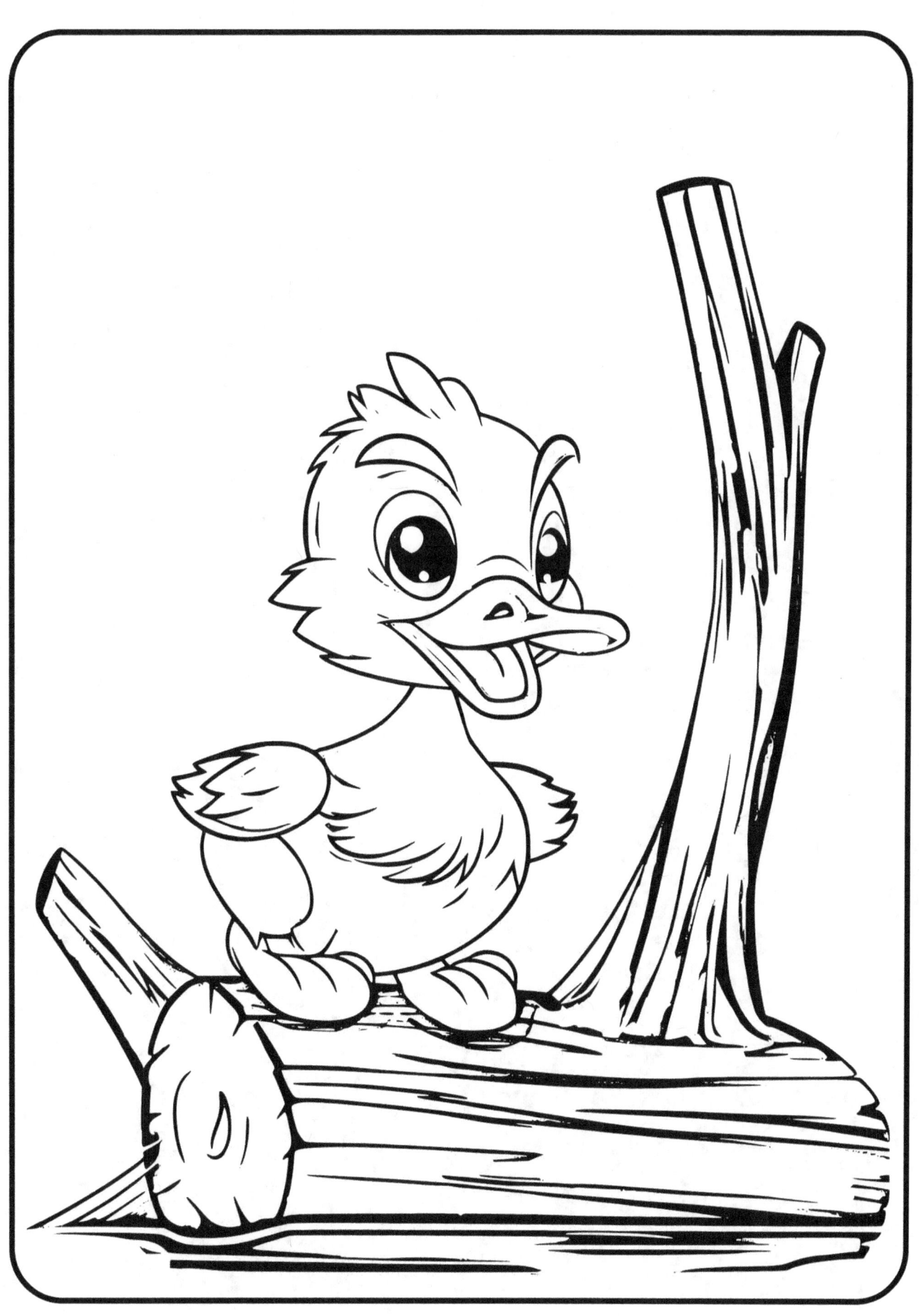

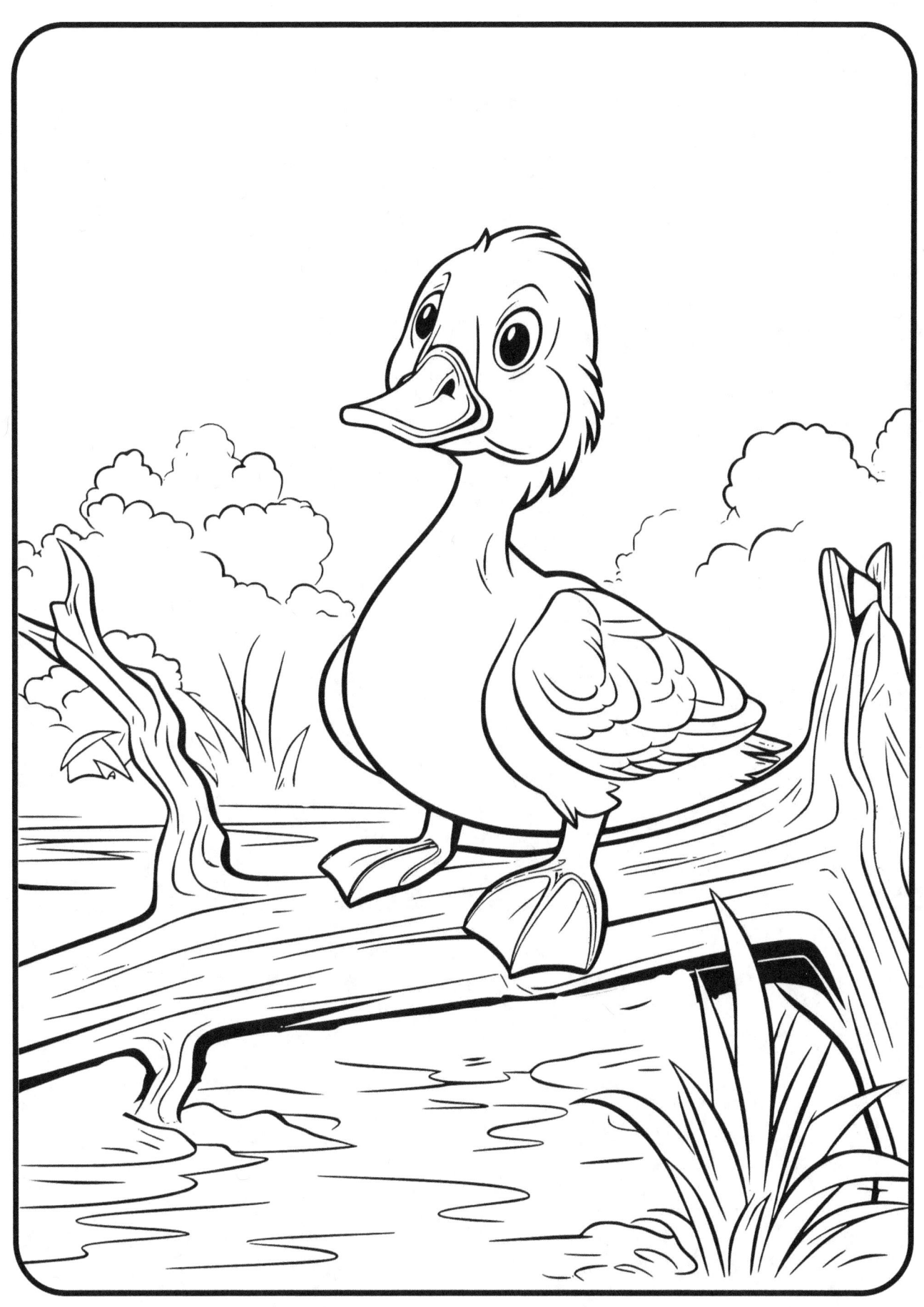

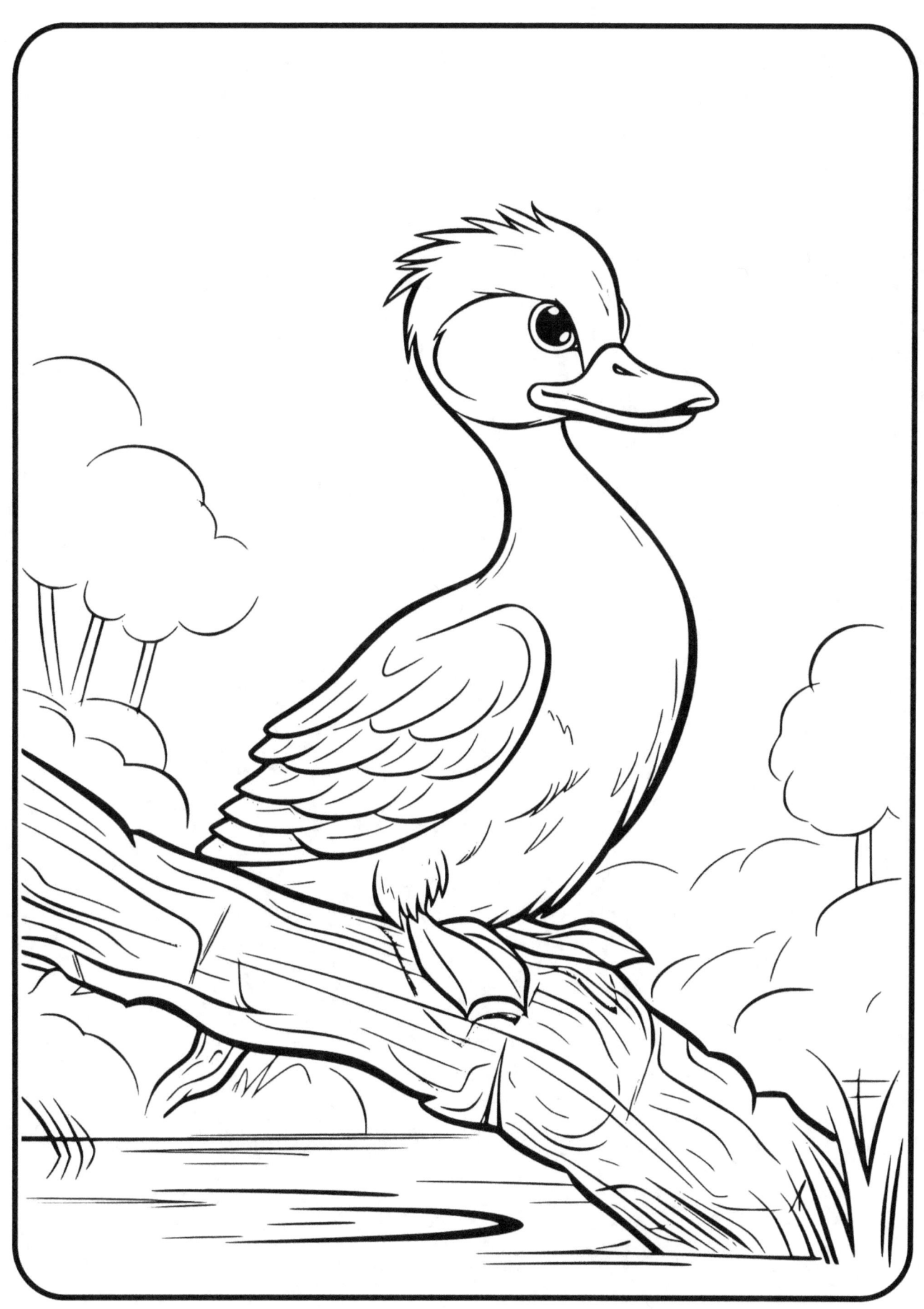

"THANK YOU FOR JOINING THIS WONDERFUL COLOR EXPEDITION WITH OUR BELOVED DUCKS! MAY EACH COLORED PAGE BE A JOYFUL AND FUN-FILLED MEMORY. WE HOPE YOU'VE ENJOYED AS MUCH AS WE HAVE!
UNTIL THE NEXT COLORFUL ADVENTURE.
GOODBYE, LITTLE ARTISTS!"